The World
100 Years Ago

The World 100 Years Ago

Michael Wynn Jones

DAVID McKAY COMPANY, INC.
NEW YORK

Title page: A picnic at Runnymeade, *c.* 1880.

First American Edition, 1976.

Picture research by Elly Beintema

Library of Congress Catalog Card Number: 76-28553
ISBN 0-679-50699-3
Printed in Great Britain

Contents

Introduction

It was the world of our great-grandfathers, and their fathers, who peer at us from behind luxuriating beards and craggy eyebrows out of brown, fading photographs. Very solemn they are, but very substantial – and confident as they pose for some homely set-piece or posture, a little mechanically, before some iron wonder of engineering. Their confidence, as we know, was not entirely misplaced: our own world is a measure of *their* achievements. We think of the twentieth century as one of dizzying social and technological change. And so it has been, but only because we are the inheritors of a generation that bequeathed, among other things, the phonograph, the typewriter, the telephone, canned foods, reinforced concrete, the bicycle, electric light, the petrol engine; that built the Suez Canal, the Mont Cenis Tunnel, the first transcontinental railroad, the first skyscraper; that produced Darwin, Edison, Mendel and Pasteur, Marx and Nietzsche.

It is tempting, perhaps, to make out an extravagant case for that age as a sort of bridgehead for the storming of the twentieth century. But that is not quite the object of this book. There is another legacy which that remarkable generation left: theirs was the first to hand down a clear and comprehensive image of their *whole* world. It was an age of intense curiosity about the planet on which they lived – not the kind of romantic or commercial curiosity that had infused earlier travellers, but an essentially scientific one. Men (and women) travelled with fixed purpose, whether in the case of the explorers and missionaries it was to bring civilization to the uninformed, or in the case of the photographers, surveyors and oceanographers to bring information back to civilization.

Out of this hardy breed *The World 100 Years Ago* is largely concerned with the exploits of the photographers. By the 1860s the pioneers of the camera had paved the way for a new skill, photo-reportage: successful photographs had been taken on the battlefield, from the tops of mountains, even from the air. It seemed as if no mere physical obstacle could stand in the way of the march of the camera, and there were plenty of adventurous spirits ready to desert the formal fantasies of the studio for the hard realities of life. There was, for instance, the indefatigable John Thomson who spent years tramping through China to bring back a unique portrait of a decaying civilization; Felice Beato, one of the first to penetrate the forbidden mysteries of Japan; Bernhard Holtermann recording the day-to-day exigencies of life in the Australian outback, and Samuel Bourne the paradoxes of British India; the Americans William Jackson and Timothy O'Sullivan, following the great surveys of the American West where no white man had walked before.

The quality of their work should not obscure the difficulties under which these pioneers laboured. Until 1880 the predominant form of photography was the wet collodion process*, an often unreliable method that encumbered the photographer with an awesome list of equipment: stereoscopic camera, lenses, camera boxes, dark tent,

---

*wet collodion method: glass plate covered with a smooth coating of collodion (a mixture of guncotton in alcohol and ether), then made light-sensitive in silver nitrate. This was placed, still wet, into a light-tight plate holder, then exposed for more than 10 seconds and developed instantaneously in pyrogallic acid, and fixed.

tripods, filters, chemicals, fixing trays, bottles, scales. It was also time-consuming, since the exposure could take anything up to a minute and a half and the processing had to be done on the spot. To complete a picture in half an hour was reckoned to be good going – even assuming that your subject had not fled before you had focussed, in the belief that the camera was about to take possession of his soul!

A few of these photographers, when they returned home, devoted themselves to long treatises on their travels and illustrated them with engravings of their pictures. But for the most part the background to *The World 100 Years Ago* is taken from the diaries and journals of their contemporaries who trod the same paths and witnessed the same events. These are an even more heterogeneous bunch, an assortment of journalists, missionaries, colonists and explorers together with a sprinkling of scholars, diplomats and tourists. Their record, naturally, is scarcely as objective as the camera's: they took with them their fixed ideas and their prejudices. But no attempt has been made to disguise them here, since this sets out to be a portrait, rather than a history, of an era.

Like all portraits it is necessarily selective. Basically it is of the decade 1870–1880, but some latitude must be allowed for the inconvenient asymmetry of history. And if some parts of the world seem to have got rather more attention at the expense of others, that is partly because they were engaged in more significant changes, and partly the shortcoming of any portrait.

Great Britain : Two Worlds

The street photographer, Clapham Common 1877.

In 1876, as an adoptive son of London, the American Henry James was perhaps the least critical of its observers. He could even be counted one of its great apologists, for ever mitigating its excesses and excusing its aberrations. 'London is so clumsy and so brutal and has gathered together so many of the darkest sides of life. . . . She is like a mighty ogress who devours human flesh,' he wrote[18]; but took pains to explain that 'the ogress herself is human. It is not in wantonness that she fills her maw, but to keep herself alive and do her tremendous work. She has no time for fine discriminations, but after all she is as good-natured as she is huge, and the more you stand up to her the better she takes the joke of it'.

The intimations of that 'tremendous work' were probably more than usually apparent to James who, at the mere sight of a sentry-box in Woolwich Barracks, was capable of summoning up 'sentiments of admiration for the greatness of England . . . a glimpse of the imperial machinery of this great country', and assumed that the local inhabitant too would 'vibrate richly, as he strolls about the breezy common of Woolwich, with all those mementoes of British dominion around him'. Well, perhaps he did if he was one of Mr Disraeli's Tory supporters; and if he were not he could scarcely be unaware of Britain's intervention in Egypt, of her annexation of the Fiji Islands, of her successful conclusion of the Ashantee War – as neat a colonial exploit as one could hope to find – and all within the space of a year.

In the train of Britain's imperial exploits came an increasing conviction of Britain's moral duty to rule an empire – a kind of divine summons to be pre-eminent over the globe, to be, as John Ruskin put it, 'for all the world a source of light, a centre of peace; mistress of learning and of the Arts, faithful guardian of time-honoured principles'. For all that many of Britain's overseas commitments had stood for generations (and in terms of history this was her second empire), in the 1870s this was a new and exciting philosophy, which occupied countless column inches in the *Pall Mall Gazette* and the *Nineteenth Century* and communicated itself to such as Henry James (who, it should be said, moved in rather more elevated circles than the wanderers of Woolwich Common).

The hub of this empire was London, with three million souls by far the greatest city on earth, with drains by Bazalgette and an underground railway that was extending itself yearly, as far as Bishopsgate and beneath the Thames. But was it a city worthy of its destiny? Gilded Prince Albert was newly enthroned on his bristling Memorial, gazing out towards the new Albert Hall, yet within a stroll of Parliament stood the shameful slums of Westminster and Seven Dials; while on its perimeter 'the low black houses as inanimate as so many rows of coalskuttles' (Mr James again) stood poised to eat up the farms of Earls Court and fields of Highgate, 'melting by wide, ugly zones into the green country'.

Quicker by bike—very probably in the crush of horse-drawn omnibuses in the City. Invented in 1865 the 'bone-shaker' pedalled bicycle reached a wide market in a very few years, even among women who sensibly adopted a more appropriate form of dress. However with its huge front driving-wheel—forerunner of the chain and gear—the 'penny-farthing' required a delicate technique, to be learned at mushrooming Bicycle Schools (centre picture) up and down the country.

More public-spirited citizens foresaw the menace of the speculator, and fought to preserve large areas of Hampstead, Wandsworth and Tooting from the omnivorous sprawl. Others sought to dignify the capital with monuments like Cleopatra's Needle (which nearly sank in the Bay of Biscay), with the vast amusement centre of Alexandra Palace (which burnt down almost immediately and had to be re-built), with the donation of Leicester Square gardens (whose benefactor very soon went bankrupt). Even the speculators, after their fashion, tried to show a concern for the environment with such aesthetic enterprises as Bedford Park. This paragon of the Queen Anne Revival (which permeated the suburbs in the 1870s), with its gables and balconies and 'antique' facings, was hailed with interest as an exercise in community planning – in a city notable for its architectural incoherence – and attracted all sorts of artistically minded families. The American steelman Andrew Carnegie, who made a special pilgrimage to see it, was, however, not so impressed[6]: 'The article in

Harper's Magazine upon Bedford Square [he meant Park] giving glowing accounts of this Arcadian colony with its aesthetic homes, its Tabard Inn and its club, made us all desire to visit it . . . Truth compels me to say we were sadly disappointed. The houses were much inferior to our preconceived ideas, and many had soft woods painted and most of the cheap shams of ordinary structures. The absence of grand trees, shady dells, and ornamental grounds, and the exceedingly cheap and cheap-looking houses made all seem like a new settlement in the Far West rather than the latest development in culture.'

Nonetheless the trend of the Queen Anne Revival persisted, and came to its fullest flowering in many of the new primary schools which were spreading across London and the whole country in the wake of the 1870 Education Act, which provided elementary education for all. These yellow-brick temples of literacy must have been as daunting to their first inmates as they are depressing today, but they suitably expressed the altruistic reforming fervour which gripped the mid-Victorians, and which, in the space of not much more than a decade, effected far-reaching reforms in the status of trade unions, the army and navy, the rights of married women, the franchise, and entry to the universities and to the Civil Service. Many of the reformers and philanthropists who found inspiration at this time are still remembered: William Booth and his army dispensing 'soup, soap and salvation' to the physically and spiritually destitute; Joseph Arch fighting for the rights of the agricultural labourer; Dr Barnardo picking up waifs off the streets of Stepney; Samuel Plimsoll inveighing against the dangers of life below decks; Elizabeth Garrett Anderson in her pioneering clinic.

And alongside these marched a legion of lesser militants, all aiming their shafts at more or less deserving targets – Early Closing Associations, Dress Reform Societies, Temperance Leagues, even Birth Controllers. Despite their variety, they by no means exhausted the huge catalogue of social injustice, some of which was too deeply embedded in the fabric of working-class life to be recognizable, or too heinous to be admitted, like child prostitution. Not until 1885, with W. T. Stead's brave crusade in the *Pall Mall Gazette*, was this particular iniquity to be exposed beyond all argument: in the meantime decent citizens preferred, as Stead put it, 'to live in a fool's paradise of imaginary innocence and purity, selfishly oblivious of the horrible realities which torment those whose lives are passed in the London Inferno'.

But they existed, these brothels full of barely-pubescent girls, most of whom had been sold to procurers by their starving parents. The going rate was £5, perhaps more for an authenticated virgin. They had to be thirteen, since that was the legal age of 'consent', but that did not mean that they had the slightest idea of what was likely

The street locksmith, one of John Thomson's scenes of London in 1877—an itinerant breed slowly being driven further into the outskirts as new roads were driven through commercial areas.

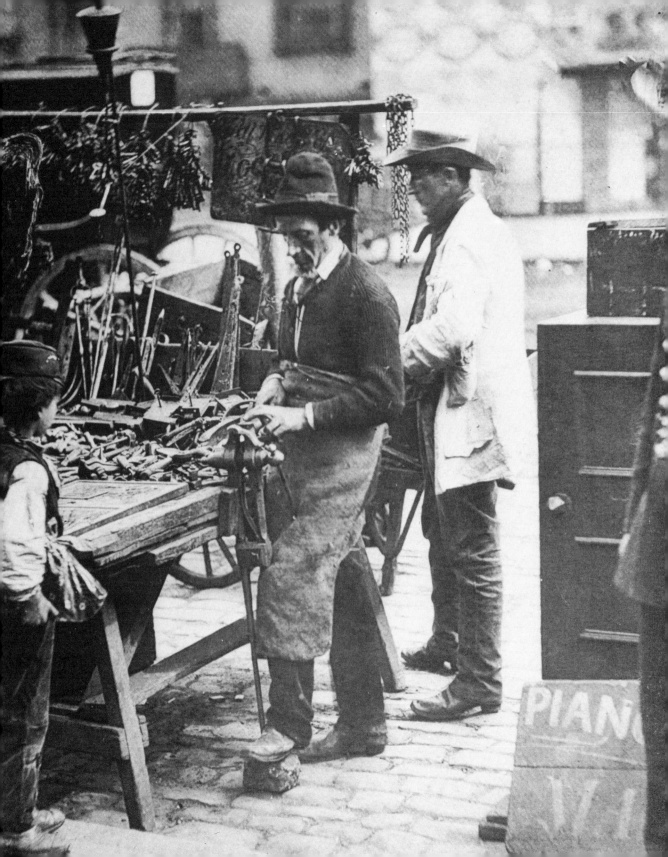

Above: London's waifs and strays on arrival at one of the Barnardo Homes (c. 1880). This charitable institution—started by Dr. Thomas Barnardo in Stepney in 1866—was one of the first to appreciate the value of photographic publicity. 'Before' pictures similar to the one above were published in brochures alongside 'after' photographs, showing the same urchins well-scrubbed and rosy-cheeked.

Right: A new literate generation: gallery class in the 1880s. W. E. Foster's Education Act of 1870, establishing board schools throughout Britain, was a landmark in the history of learning. For the first time a free primary education was universally available—in theory at least. It took another two decades for the system to be fully implemented and proper schools to be built.

Left: The Sanitary Men, 1877: public employees whose job it was to 'disinfect' houses where a case of smallpox (still a recurring scourge of London) was notified. This they did by removing all contaminated clothes, bedding etc. to be heated up in a special oven.

to happen to them at the hands of their 'clients' or, for that matter, what *had* happened to them after they'd finished. 'The maiden tribute of Modern Babylon', snorted the *Pall Mall Gazette*; but then only marginally better off were those respectable girls exploited by the sweat-shops of the City.

'I take my stand in the dreary twilight of a winter's early morning on Blackfriars or London bridge,' wrote an anonymous observer of the London scene in 1878[43], 'and I see trooping past me, in such numbers that the wide pavement is thickly occupied, girls ranging from thirteen to seventeen . . . They are not ragged girls by any means – a little tawdry maybe as regards their beflounced skirts and gay hats, not so substantially shod as the freezing slush of the pavement makes desirable.' They are bound, he learns, for factories across the river where, for a pittance of 7s a week, they would work for twelve or thirteen hours a day, sometimes never seeing the daylight, and for lunch eating their 'pennyworth of vilely cooked vegetables with plate on lap, in the same tainted atmosphere they and their fifty companions have all morning been breathing'.

It was small wonder if, like so many others, they turned later to drink as a temporary refuge from the brutal routine. No one disputed that drunkenness was the besetting vice of the nation: nor did one have to frequent the back-alleys and gin-palaces of the city to reach that conclusion for oneself. 'Our laundry did not come on the day it was due, nor on the next day nor the day after that,' peeved the French writer and critic Hippolyte Taine on one of his several stays in London. 'The laundryman tells us that his laundresses have been drunk all week. Since I got here I have seen three women drunk in the streets. Two near Hyde Park, in the most handsome street in the city, were obviously women of easy virtue of the lowest class ... the third, a decently dressed woman of fifty, was reeling about in the midst of a small crowd and admitted that she was drunk. I believe this vice to be very rare among well bred women; however, extreme boredom or grief may lead some to it. On the other hand, drunkenness among the people is terrible. During the last few days I have twice been down to Chelsea and both times came across men lying dead drunk on the pavement. My friend who lives in that district often finds working girls and women in the same condition ...'

In this fertile soil the Total Abstinence societies prospered greatly. Their posters – the devil presiding over a stupefied drunkard, as his attendant imps removed the sorry man's heart and brain in shovelfuls – were to be seen on every street corner, though their little blue lapel-ribbons (indicating the wearer had taken the pledge) were not quite so much in evidence. If, however, it was boredom, or grief as M. Taine so charitably suggested, that drove the better class of lady to drink, that perhaps was understandable. The life of a young lady was

Below: Formal family pose at Broom House, Fulham in the 1860s (before the decline of the crinoline). A characteristic upper middle-class drawing room, in which cluttered, brocaded mid-Victorian taste has been grafted on to Georgian classicism.

The wrong side of Paradise: Drury Lane in the 1870s, a slum within a stone's throw of the busy and prosperous Strand. One refuge for the destitute was Baylis's restaurant (left), above which were let cheap rooms for ex-convicts. Others (above) lacked so much as a roof over their heads, driven to begging even off the poor. The 'crawlers' of St Giles, they were called, like the old lady in the photograph (1875), child-minding for a cup of tea and the prospect of a scrap of bread.

generally vacuous, circumscribed by social conventions as rigid as the whalebone stays beneath her crinoline – as we can discern from the youthful journals of Laura Troubridge[32]. 'Monday, October 26, 1873: I was thinking the other day how I should spend my day if I was allowed to do as I liked and if it was possible. I would not be *idle* – on the contrary *very* industrious . . .'

But there were hopeful (or ominous, depending on your point of view) signs for those who cared to heed them. The crinoline was fast giving way to the bustle, still a complex jungle of wires, but less inhibiting and infinitely more erotic. Lawn tennis was rapidly outstripping croquet as a pastime fit for the fairer sex; roller-skating had become something of a craze, and bicycling held all sorts of giddy possibilities (not least of a revolution in underwear). No longer was it considered prudent for a lady novelist to disguise herself as George, nor to refrain from voicing serious opinions on matters of politics or art – though Messrs Holman Hunt and Millais might have revised that opinion had they read some of young Laura's entries in her diary: 'Our February half-holiday was very jolly for it came just in the strongest time of a new rage. It was for painting the panels of the shutters of our bedrooms, such fun to do; you can't think how pre-Raph. they look. Pale blue ground, oils – you know – quite grand, and in each panel droops a flower, of course very pre-Raphly done.'

In fact Laura Troubridge soon grew into an accomplished artist and became acquainted with Oscar Wilde, already the *enfant terrible* of the Aesthetic Movement: 'July 1879; went to tea at Oscar Wilde's – great fun, lots of vague 'intense' men, such duffers, who amused us awfully. The room was a mass of white lilies, photoes of Mrs Langtry, peacock feather screens and coloured pots, pictures of various merit.' Laura was not a retiring lady by nature, but other women had also taken heart from John Stuart Mill's *The Subjection of Women* (1869), and were actively campaigning for their 'emancipation' (which was the current jargon). There had been notable successes – two women's colleges had been founded at Cambridge, and by the middle of the decade, after initial resistance, women were admitted to teaching hospitals to study medicine. There were hopes, too, that the vocal minority in Parliament who declared themselves in favour of female suffrage must soon accomplish something.

Such hopes proved to be premature. Too many men recoiled from Tennyson's vision of strapping womanhood (which the ladies of Girton College did nothing to diminish when they formed their own fire brigade and organized their own rowing eight), and even other women – like the redoubtable Mrs Sutherland Orr[23] – publicly announced that things had gone far enough: 'the one fatal result of female emancipation is this, that in its full and final attainment not only the power of love in women, but for either sex its possibility, will have passed away.' It would result, she said, in 'the decomposition

Standing room only: the problems of transporting one's wardrobe in the 1860s. The complicated infra-structure of a crinoline is unloaded off a knifeboard bus in Sloane Street, London. With the advent of the bustle in the late 1860s such practical problems were mitigated at least, if not entirely solved.

All the rage: the aesthetic way
to have your photograph taken in the 1870s.
A pre-Raphaelite portrait composition by
Julia Margaret Cameron.

of society'; to which the suffragist Millicent Fawcett scornfully replied that these gloomy prophecies had not the slightest foundation in fact.

Even if the prospect of society's decomposition was somewhat far-fetched, it was nevertheless a potent threat to make to an Establishment founded on the bedrock principles of the British way of life. Whatever tended to cause that way of life to 'decompose' – dissent, divorce, free thought – was anathema; whatever sustained or strengthened it – education, free trade, self-help – was patriotic. All progress or reform had to be measured by these criteria, and it really didn't do to tamper too rapidly or too radically with the structures of society. A self-made man was not begrudged his advancement, provided he adopted the rules of his new caste – Charles Bradlaugh was not ostracized because he had risen from wharf clerk to Member of Parliament, but because when he got there he doggedly refused to take the oath.

In consequence there were two distinct Londons, characterized even in those days as Paradise and Inferno – no different perhaps from all large cities, but here on a much larger scale and certainly more in evidence: the fashionable eating-houses of Greenwich (where politicians still repaired for the annual Whitebait Feast at the end of the session) were well within sniffing-distance of the debris of Wapping Steps; the great thoroughfare of the Strand led directly to the hovels of Drury Lane, and the Devil's Acre mouldered in the very shadow of the Abbey.

It was precisely this uneasy co-existence that fascinated the French artist, Gustave Doré, and his companion Blanchard Jerrold, when they came to make their 'pilgrimage' to London (the results of which they published in 1872[8]). Doré's engravings vividly capture the spirit of Dickens's city (who had, after all, only died in 1870) – the oases of gaslight, the choking fogs 'rolling into the houses like a feather bed', the Refuges out of which echoed the crackling coughs 'like the distant running fire of musketry', and the animated chaos of rat-infested docks. But here, too, is the London of Trollope, where somehow the sun manages to penetrate to illumine the smart horses clipping down Ladies' Mile, the elegantly circulating fêtes of Chiswick Gardens, the bonnetted parades of Hyde Park.

Rarely in his illustrations do the two Londons meet. To be sure, the two pilgrims note, in their dress the poor ape the rich: 'An English crowd is almost the ugliest in the world, because the poorer classes are but copyists in costume . . . The English carpenter wears a black tail coat – like the waiter, the undertaker, and the duke. Poor English women are ghastly in their patches trimmed in outlandish imitation of the fashion . . . Observe this lemonade-vendor. His dress is that of a prosperous middle-class man, gone to shreds and patches.'

And yet, one feels, their sympathies are really with the poor and

their ability to snatch enjoyment in the teeth of despair: their bank-holiday fairs, their oyster-stalls and music halls. For indeed, 'we are now in the Music Hall and Refreshment Bar epoch: an epoch of much gilding and abundant looking-glass – as, on the stage, we are in the era of spangles and burlesque . . . The example of the West is, as I have observed, tending eastward and penetrating the lowest of the population. The Cambridge Music Hall is superseding the penny gaff and the sing-song at the thief's public-house. In the City the cavernous drinking-places are dying out – before the gilded glories of Crosby Hall. It is a lighter time than our fathers', that in which we live.'

Twice in the year, according to Doré, the two Londons came together – both occasions devoted to that most British of diversions, physical contest. The Boat Race, between the university crews of Oxford and Cambridge, was 'a holiday for all London: for Parliament and people, for the Heir Apparent planted in the Umpire's boat and for the workfolk lining the sylvan shores'. Puzzling though it might have been to a Frenchman to find total strangers taking passionate sides for the day between two sets of upper-class toffs, he nonetheless rejoiced in the spectacle. 'The vibration of vigorous human life that thrilled along the shores on that April day was not that of a mournful, dejected population,' declared Jerrold. 'The towing paths presented to the view of the more fortunate people upon the private riverside terraces, a mixed population that, in its holiday guise, showed marks of the fierce London struggle. The mechanics and their wives and children looked pale; but they were of buoyant spirits.'

'Why are those urchins perched up in yonder limes so utterly possessed with the keen spirit of the day?' mused the Frenchman. 'Why is the gipsy lad proud of the pale blue in his straw hat? Why are those groups of poor shopmen wrangling over the relative merits of the Cambridge and Oxford stroke? Why is there a sparkle in the eyes of the servant girls and the street-folk generally?'

His English companion ponders these mysteries and decides 'It is the race of life, in little . . . It is the combativeness which lies deep in the English nature: and which has expressed itself in brutal and in noble forms ever since we were a nation'. This is what binds all classes of society, however ephemerally: it is even the dynamic behind Britain's imperial drive, he seems to suggest. 'This same spirit is that which has developed our unparalleled extent of trade . . . [and incidentally] leads all classes of Englishman to the race-course.'

For that is the other excursion which brought all Londoners, regardless of their station, together: the Derby. Even Henry James hoisted himself to the top of an omnibus to sample this communal excitement. 'You perceive you are in for the vulgar on an unsurpassable scale, something blatantly, unimaginable, heroically shocking to timid taste,' he explained with a little *frisson* of anticipation. 'You get

Recruiting sergeants lying in wait outside a public house, 1876. Impeccably turned out and almost avuncular, they were experts at catching the eye, and the curiosity, of any likely lad half-tempted to take the Queen's shilling.

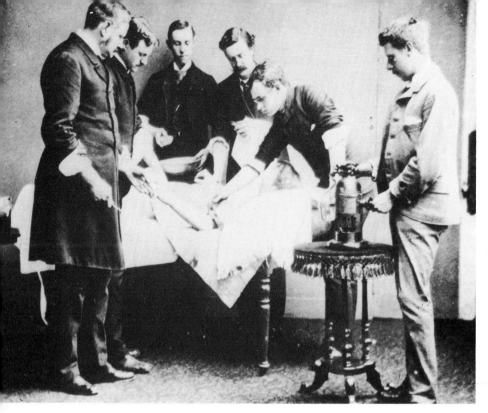

Left: A surgical operation in progress in 1869, two years after Joseph Lister's epoch-making announcement of the practice of antiseptic surgery using carbolic acid. The universal adoption of his methods, as demonstrated here, helped to eliminate the ever-present risk of gangrene from the operating theatre.

for the first time a notion of the London population at large. It has piled itself into carts, into omnibuses, into every possible and impossible species of trap. A large proportion of it, of course, is on foot, trudging along the perilous margin of the middle way in such comfort as maybe gathered from fifteen miles' dodging of broken shins. The smaller the vehicle, the more rat-like the animal that drags it, the more numerous and ponderous its human freight'.

James counts, with astonishment, the number of wayside halts on the road to Epsom; he notes the 'verdant if cockneyfied common of Clapham ranged with commodious houses of sober red complexion, from under whose neo-classic pediments you expect to see a mild-faced lady emerge, distributing tracts from a green silk satchel'. He marvels in the kaleidoscopic panorama of the Downs, 'nigger-minstrels and beggars and mountebanks and spangled persons on stilts and gipsy matrons . . . free-handed youths and young ladies with gilded hair . . . gentlemen in pairs, mounted on stools, habited in fantastic sporting garments and offering bets to whomsoever listed', and who, apparently, found plenty of patrons among 'the baser sort'. Above all, it reminded him (as it did Gustave Doré) that 'the dusky vistas of the London residential streets are not a complete symbol of the complicated race that erected them.'

If this was a momentary escape from the Inferno for the working class, perhaps it was also a welcome reprieve for some from Paradise, too. The diversity of social situation of the multiplying middle classes – so genteelly summed up for us today in the cartoons of Du Maurier, in the decorous covers of songsheets, in picture postcards of faintly absurd bathing-machines – was here disguised. For some this form of paradise was a destination securely arrived at, for others it was, at best, a waiting-stage of hopes and aspirations.

Yet there were areas of London where the effort not to sink back into the Inferno was all too apparent. 'Do you know Camden Town?' asked our anonymous observer. 'A sweet spot: the home, *par excellence*, of the commercial clerk of from 30s a week to two-fifty a year – an estimable, responsible, hard-working man. Houses all built to meet the requirements of the clerkly world; they even look as if they had been manufactured of dingy blotting-paper, and are so fragile they could be taken out with an eraser. Thoroughly respectable though: none of your low lodgings, or anything of that sort! Nice parlour, wire blind in the window; very shiny, sticky, gummy furniture; chairs with American-cloth seats which stick to your trousers; vase with everlasting flowers, and two china dogs on mantelpiece . . . a black-beetly kitchen where Maria Jane cooks everything with coal garnish and soot sauce: and bedrooms which are well described as airy.'

At the affluent end, in the substantial households of Cavendish

Below: The annual exhibition of the Royal Photographic Society of Great Britain, on the twenty-first anniversary of its foundation. In its lifetime the society had witnessed the transition from the cumbersome wet collodion process to dry plate photography (in general use by the early eighties).

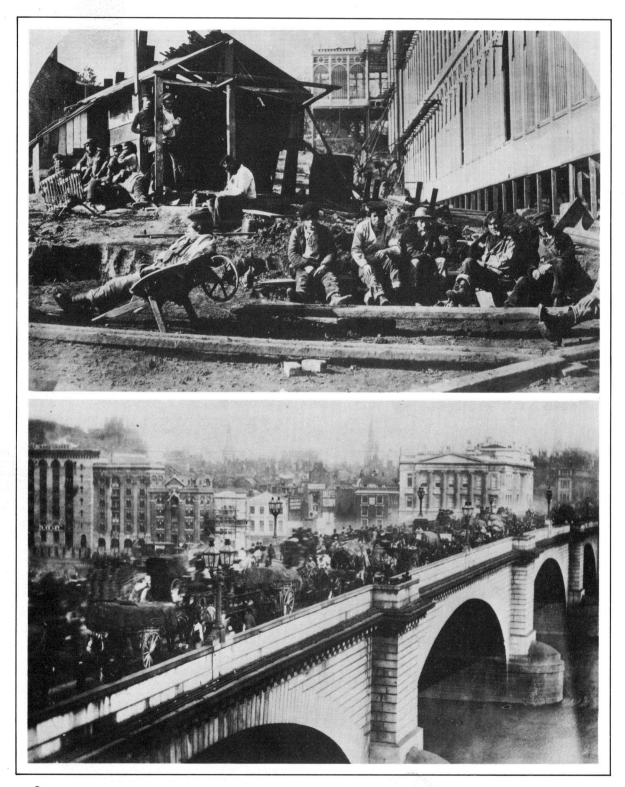

Above left: Crystal Palace re-erected on its permanent site at Sydenham Hill. Though a product of the 1850s Joseph Paxton's pioneering structure of glass and iron exerted a profound influence on the architecture of the next two decades – in particular on the huge hemisphere of St. Pancras station (built 1869). Below left: Looking north across London Bridge in the 1870s. A hundred years has done little to improve the problems of rush-hour traffic. Right: Divers at work on Blackfriars Bridge. The new bridge across the Thames, replacing Mylne's old structure of 1760, was completed in 1869.

Square or Cheyne Walk, life was comfortably insulated with coal-fires, Venetian blinds, morning and evening prayers, and speaking-tubes down to the servants' hall – where butler, footman, groom and gardener, cook housekeeper, nurse, housemaid and kitchen maid, between-maid and under-housemaid (who actually expected to earn £12 a year for her exertions!) were all awaiting the summons. 'Remember,' enjoined a contemporary ladies' magazine, 'to be careful of a servant's health and comfort; but indulgence is not apt to improve her health, temper or manners. It is a wicked maxim that "anything will do for the servants", and equally unwise to pamper foibles, or give too much liberty or licence of speech.' In such an august establishment, a simple dinner-party could hardly get away with less than: soups, water-souchet of flounders, stewed eels, curried lobster, salmon pudding, broiled trout with sweet herbs, devilled whitebait. And that was just for starters. From there the menu would make its ponderous (and, very likely, indigestible) way through at least fifteen other offerings, finishing up, no doubt, with one of those cumbrous boiled puddings so popular up at the Palace.

A Londoner, northward bound in the 1870s, passing through Scott's towering Gothic shrine at St Pancras and on into the mighty glass-and-iron hemisphere beyond, could have been left in no doubt as to the railways' place in the Victorian scheme of things. They had passed in the previous two decades through their 'heroic age' (when more than 15,000 miles of track had been laid) to reach their apotheosis in 1872 with the last brick of this terminal-shrine. Not everyone, of course, shared in the genuflecting. John Ruskin wrote crossly: 'Now every fool in Buxton can be in Bakewell in half an hour, and every fool in Bakewell at Buxton; which you think a lucrative process of exchange – you Fools Everywhere!' (which was as much a reflection of his concern for the refined delights of Buxton as a quiet spa as of his general antipathy for railways). And the Anti-Sunday Travel Union was hard at work – especially in Scotland – attempting to stem the tide of the nation's moral degeneration.

By the beginning of the decade, however, Britain could boast a very complete national railway network – and a multiplicity of competing companies (not all of whom could agree on a standard gauge) – so that to conduct his 'Rambles beyond Railways', Wilkie Collins was obliged to penetrate some quite desolate areas. Many far-reaching effects of the iron road were already being felt: new ports, like Barrow and Grimsby, were springing up out of almost nothing, while others, ill-served by the new god, were decaying rapidly. Unfamiliar building materials, like Welsh slate, were germinating everywhere, even in the dormitory settlements for the new 'commuter' which huddled round country stations outside big cities. It was a mixed blessing: the Manchester businessman was delighted to be able to

End of an era: the fast-disappearing four-in-hand, outside the Ship Inn at Porlock in Somerset, in the late 1860s.

Left: The gentle pursuit of Sphairistike, 'invented' by Wingfield in 1874 and refined into the sport of lawn tennis, photographed in a country garden in 1878. The previous year the first Wimbledon championships had been held. Inset: Cycles for all sizes: a family cycling 'club' – note the badges and uniform – posing with their penny-farthings in 1870. Croquet (below) remained unchallenged on vicarage lawns, and modesty prevailed on Britain's beaches (right) with head-to-toe bathing dresses.

buy his London paper at ten o'clock in the morning, but the country inn-keeper would hardly have shared his enthusiasm as he watched his coach-trade fading away.

Not that the inns had yet entirely succumbed to the march of progress. For his expedition from Brighton to his ancestral home in Dunfermline, Andrew Carnegie preferred to hire a four-in-hand (pronouncing it – strangely for one of the leaders of the new technology – 'an incomparable mode of travel') and found ample well-appointed hostelries for his party. Hippolyte Taine, too, travelling by train from York to London during his tour of Britain (at an average speed of only twenty m.p.h.), complained that 'in the speed of the travelling all these sights pass through the mind like so much stage scenery', and vowed that only a very lively taste for travel could reconcile anyone to the profound discomforts of the third-class.

But Britain was contracting rapidly, for better or worse, and for the insatiably curious – like Henry James – it opened up irresistible horizons. Diligent study of Mr Bradshaw's timetables took him (first-class of course) to Devon, 'the perfection of the rural picturesque . . . from the carriage window a veritable landscape in water colours', to the country houses of Warwickshire, where 'the cushiony lawns afforded to a number of very amiable people an opportunity of playing lawn tennis. . . . These young ladies kept the ball going with an agility worthy of the sisters and sweethearts of a race of cricketers and gave me a chance to admire their flexibility of figure and their freedom of action. They might have passed for the attendant nymphs of Diana . . . there had indeed been a chance for them to wear the quiver, a target for archery being erected on the lawn.' And to Oxford (Jowett's new progressive Oxford) for a degree ceremony, where he was shocked to witness 'the boisterous conduct of the students, who superabound in extravagant applause, in impertinent interrogation and in lively disparagement of the orator's Latinity.'

The railways could also transport you to less ethereal regions. To 'slag-heaps like mountains, the earth deformed by excavation, and tall flaming furnaces', as M. Taine discovered. 'Manchester: a sky turned coppery red by the setting sun; a cloud strangely shaped resting upon the plain; and under this motionless cover a bristling of chimneys by hundreds, all tall as obelisks. Then a mass, a heap, blackish, enormous, endless rows of buildings; and you are there, at the heart of a Babel built of brick.' Closer investigation simply confirms the sordid picture. 'One of the factory blocks is a rectangle six storeys high, each storey having forty windows: and inside, lit by gas-jets and deafened by the uproar of their own labour, toil thousands of workmen, penned in, regimented, hands active, feet motionless, all day and every day, mechanically serving their machines. Could there be any kind of life more outraged, more opposed to man's natural instincts?'

Above: Switchboard operators at Manchester's first telephone exchange, early 1880s. London installed its first exchange in 1879. Below: More traditional means of communication: mending a cobbled road in Oxford, photographed by Henry Taunt whose premises appear in the background.

Left: The jet workshop at Whitby, on
the Yorkshire coast, photographed by
Frank Sutcliffe. Here the local
semi-precious stone was brought to be
carved and polished by craftsmen.
Above: The sunless slums of Glasgow
in the late 1860s: Annan's portrait of
Gallowgate.

Relentlessly Taine pursues his quest. 'At about six o'clock the factories discharge an excited, noisy crowd into the streets . . . a number of them stop at the gin-shops, the rest scatter to their lairs. We follow them: what dreary streets! Through half-open windows we could see wretched rooms at ground level, or often below the damp earth's surface. Masses of livid children, dirty and flabby of flesh, crowd each threshold and breathe the vile air of the street, less vile than within.'

Liverpool, equally, is a monster but salvaged by its docks and its promise of freedom. 'One ship lying at anchor, the *Great Britain*, was about to sail for Australia with twelve hundred emigrants . . . sailing-ships glide down the river, bowing, supple, beautiful as swans. The ninety-gun man-o'-war *George*, with both sails and steam, arrives in harbour like a sovereign, all that crowd of shipping making way for her.' But then, behind all this is Leeds Street, where 'every stairway swarms with children; their faces are pale, their hair whitish and tousled, the rags they wear are full of holes, they have neither shoes nor stockings and they are all vilely dirty. . . . Some of the tiniest children are still fresh and rosy-cheeked, but it hurts to look at their great blue eyes; for that clear healthy blood is going to be spoilt, and you see scrofulous little faces marred by small open sores covered with a piece of paper.'

The divorce of families such as these from any contact with nature was by now total, yet the industrial centres continued to be a magnet for the one class which was even worse off, the agricultural labourer. The spread of Fenian outrages from across the water to England at the end of the sixties had served to remind people that there remained a desperate agrarian problem in Ireland, but it had tended to divert attention from the fact that conditions in the countryside at home were hardly better. The steady trickle of concern, official and charitable, for the industrial worker – which manifested itself in legislation on the right to strike, in mechanics' institutes, free libraries, philanthropic settlements, educational associations – seemed to dry up before it reached the tillers of the soil. Indeed the general attitude towards the farm-worker was curiously churlish. 'Hodge' he was invariably designated by *Punch*, a besmocked simpleton with straw in his hair. Horny-handed and witless, he was still not considered worthy of the vote which had, in 1867, been bestowed on urban workers. Taine found him courteous, more careful of his appearance than French peasants, but 'drawn, strained, sad and humble'. He was appalled to inspect his cottage: 'wattle and daub with thatched roof, the rooms too low and too small, the interior walls too thin. Think of a large family crowded into two such rooms in winter, with clothes drying on them . . .' He found the womenfolk with 'haggard faces blotchily red, and a wasted, exhausted look', either from the bearing of too many children or from labouring in the fields to supplement

Rural England: thousands deserted the land during the depression that persisted well into the 1880s, but harvest-time (above) was an occasion for the whole village to turn out. The test of a good farmer was a solid 'heavy' stack of hay (below) that could be sliced 'straight as a table-top' to provide trusses.

their husbands' miserable eight shillings a week.

It was uncritically assumed, in the corridors of Whitehall and the smoking-room of the Athenaeum, that those who worked on the land could live by the land; but Hodge, had he divined this, would have respectfully pointed out that a century and a half of enclosure acts had wrung the last vestiges of smallholding from the villagers. In the 1870s he was just a day-labourer, who at that was only called upon to labour on fine days. Everything conspired to drive him from the land, a succession of wet and miserable seasons, the creeping insolvency of tithe-ridden farmers and, above all, the advent of massive imports of prairie wheat from America and frozen meats from the Antipodes. By the time the agricultural depression had waned in the mid-eighties, more than a million acres of land had been lost to wheat, and over a hundred thousand labourers departed to seek salvation in the slums.

There were indeed protests, like the dogged six-month strike of workers in East Anglia in 1874. But the days were gone when conditions on the land could inspire the terrorism of a 'Captain Swing' and his bands of arsonists, just as the day was yet to dawn when the trades unions could be talked of openly as a political threat. Britain in the 1870s was shaken by no convulsions, no dangerous social experiments and no serious blows to her esteem abroad. It was a moment to be proud, when every third ship on the ocean was British-registered and when the iron and steel industries of France, Germany and America combined could not match half our production. It was a moment to be supremely self-confident, when the moral fibre of the country could sustain High Anglicanism *and* Evolution, and its parliamentary system could embrace both the flamboyant Disraeli and the grandiloquent Gladstone. It was a moment to be – well, perhaps a little complacent?

After the decade had passed, the radical Frederic Harrison penned a few tongue-in-cheek words on the subject to *The Fortnightly Review*.

Surely no century in all human history was ever so much praised to its face for its wonderful achievements, its wealth and its power, its unparalleled ingenuity and its miraculous capacity for making itself comfortable and generally enjoying life. British Associations, and all sorts of associations, economic, scientific and mechanical, are perpetually executing cantatas in honour of the age of progress. . . . The gentlemen who perform wonderful and unsavoury feats in crowded lecture halls always remind us that 'Never was such a time as this nineteenth century!' Public men laying the first stones of institutes, museums, or amusing the Royal Academy after dinner, great inventors who have reaped fortunes and titles, raise up their hands and bless us in the benignity of affluent old age. . . . The journals perform the part of orchestra, banging big drums and blowing trumpets – penny trumpets, twopenny, threepenny, or sixpenny trumpets.

As a mere mite in this magnificent epoch, I ask myself, What have I done, and many plain people round me, who have no mechanical genius at all – what have we done to deserve this perpetual cataract of congratulation?

'Boardie Willie' advertises the attractions of the Westcliffe Saloon, by Frank Sutcliffe.

Europe: Revolution & Reaction

Paris: the Bois de Boulogne in more peaceful times.

On 1 April 1867, to the music of Offenbach and with the Champ-de-Mars translated into one enormous pleasure-park, Napoleon III and his Empress, Eugénie, declared open their spectacular World Fair. It was a display worthy of Haussmann's new and magnificently boulevarded city: a monumental pageant of human achievement, from thirteenth-century tapestries and Japanese prints to the latest railway engine from Britain. How becoming that all these wonders should have been assembled under the auspices of another of the world's great achievements, Napoleon's glittering Second Empire! All the world came to Paris that summer, William of Prussia and Bismarck, his Chancellor, the Sultan of Turkey, Tsar Alexander II (who narrowly avoided being shot there), the Prince of Wales, kings, queens, pashas and presidents. Mark Twain was there, too, one of the Innocents en route for the Holy Land[34], absorbed by his glimpse of his Imperial Majesty: 'a long-bodied, short-legged man, fiercely moustached, old, wrinkled, with eyes half-closed, and *such* a deep, crafty, scheming expression about them! Napoleon, bowing ever so gently to the loud plaudits, and watching every thing and every body with his cat-eyes from under his depressed hatbrim, as if to discover any sign that those cheers were not heartfelt and cordial.'

Well might Napoleon have peered suspiciously at his subjects. Who would have thought that in just over three years they would disown him utterly, desperately ill and a helpless prisoner of Prussia? Or that the splendours of the Empire, and all its sparkling *demi-mondaines*, would have been snuffed out in a welter of blood? But there were omens – the clandestine anti-Bonapartist clubs, the undertow of booing beneath all the applause. And there was one omen so gigantic that anyone could have overlooked it: it stood in the centre of the Champ-de-Mars, Herr Krupp's fifty-ton cannon which fired 1,000-pound shells and dwarfed every known firearm in the world into insignificance.

This monstrous product from across the Rhine was something of a puzzle. It was recognized that Germany had progressed by leaps and bounds since the days of its princelings whose main assets were their subjects, whom they sold as mercenaries to pay for their grandiose opera-houses. It was known that Count Bismarck, known also for his taste for herrings, had created under the leadership of Prussia a federation of states, which had proved capable of putting Denmark in its place and, just recently, had despatched the vaunted armies of the Habsburg Empire in a matter of seven weeks. But this juggernaut of iron was, surely, wishful thinking? Herr Pumpernickel, as the normally sedate *Times* called him, was getting above his station. Had it been known that, even at that moment, teams of surveyors were mapping the region around Metz with a view to the possible construction of railway supply lines, certain opinions might have been hastily revised.

A clash between the two major Continental powers was inevitable – if only because Bismarck desired it as the culmination of his 'imperial' German policy, and quixotic elements in France declared themselves ready for it (though not the Emperor, for all his faith in his Zouaves and Chasseurs, his chassepot rifles and *mitrailleuses*, or embryonic machine-guns). The excuse came in the summer of 1870 – even as the British Foreign Secretary was scanning the diplomatic horizon and perceiving 'no cloud in the sky' – and it came from a source that was more reminiscent of eighteenth-century diplomacy than that of the nineteenth. On 2 June news reached France that the Spanish throne, vacant since the abdication of Isabella, had been offered to Prince Leopold of Hohenzollern – to a kinsman of the Prussian king and a full-blooded German cavalry officer to boot. Clearly, it was unthinkable that France should suffer potentially hostile regimes on two fronts, as Leopold must have realised: his initial acceptance was withdrawn.

That should have been more than enough for French esteem, and perhaps would have been, but for an arrogant aristocrat in the Foreign Ministry, the Duke of Gramont, who insisted that honour demanded an assurance from William of Prussia that the candidature would never be renewed. To William this appeared a quite superfluous undertaking, as he informed the French ambassador, refusing to prolong discussion on the subject. The king replied to Napoleon

Above: The political puppet-master of Europe: Count Bismarck (mounted, far right) relaxes with his hounds on his estate at Vlashin.

to that effect in a telegram – the infamous Ems Telegram. This passed on its way through Count Bismarck's hands and in the process underwent a subtle change of wording, which implied that the French ambassador had been summarily dismissed.

Bismarck had calculated French reaction very precisely. On 15 July France declared war on Prussia 'on a point of etiquette', as *The Illustrated London News* so appropriately put it. In the streets of Paris frenetic crowds chanted 'La Marseillaise' and raised the cry '*à Berlin!*': along the floodlit Unter den Linden and around the Brandenburg Gate, only slightly less histrionic crowds intoned the National Anthem and cheered '*nach Paris!*' And there the similarity ended, for at once the Prussian military machine (as nurtured by Moltke and von Roon) revealed itself as the most meticulously organized in the world, mobilizing over a million men to the colours within eighteen days, while French reservists wandered the length and breadth of their country in search of their units. France had embarked on her most disastrous and humiliating war.

It all happened with disorientating speed. By the end of August one French army under Marshal MacMahon had been defeated at Worth (6 August) and another under Bazaine had been caught at Gravelotte, as it attempted to fall back on Verdun (18 August). Here, the slaughter on both sides was terrible, but as night fell

Below: The Papal troops in St Peter's Square, Rome, July 1870, receive the papal benediction. Most of those present were French troops supplied by Napoleon III for the protection of the Pope, but now summoned back to France on the eve of the Franco-Prussian war. Their evacuation opened the way for the final act of Italian Unification, the fall of Rome.

Bazaine was forced to seek shelter in the 'impregnable' fortress of Metz, which was promptly put under siege. Now, between nearly a quarter of a million advancing Germans and Paris, stood just 100,000 Frenchmen under MacMahon (and Napoleon, less concerned now with '*la gloire*' than with his wife's injunction to do '*son devoir*'), dug in around the citadel of Sedan. At six o'clock on the morning of 1 September, as the mist was lifting from the valley of the Meuse, the Bavarian guns opened up, and presently wave on wave of Prussian infantry were emerging from the woods, closing one escape route after another. The French army was assuredly, in the immemorial words of one of its commanders, 'in a chamber-pot about to be shitted upon'. No amount of desperate and reckless cavalry charges could break the stranglehold, and by five in the afternoon when the last batteries fell silent, no one doubted the outcome.

A *Daily News* correspondent[7] watched the Emperor drive off grimly to the German lines the next morning to surrender his royal person, 'pale and anxious-looking, with his face set firm . . . he glances from the carriage window and bows in return to the stranger who has raised his hat to the fallen Emperor. There are few who raise their hats . . . I judge by their muttered remarks that the greater part of them are decidedly anti-Imperialist now. The prisoners are even stronger in their language. They have been ruined by imbeciles. Their generals ought to be shot. They have been betrayed.'

Two days later, in Paris, a resident described the stunned reception of the news, then the gradual awakening, the hurried meetings of ministers, the placards on the walls, Jules Favre declaring the '*déchéance*' (abdication), the National Guard swarming on to the streets hailing the Republic. 'Such perfect unanimity I never witnessed. As it is Sunday, the people are walking about with their wives and children in holiday dress. The *Gardes Nationales* are marching home along the boulevards as though they had come from a review. The windows and the pavements are lined with people cheering them. It is felt by all that the surrender of the Chief of State must be repudiated by the nation; that it has been repudiated; and that the dishonour falls consequently on the man, and not on France.'

Soon the Germans were to learn that while the war with the Emperor was over, the war with the people was just beginning. Not that it troubled them overmuch: the investment of Paris, where all available soldiers, sheep, cows and chickens had been commandeered, went ahead with ruthless efficiency. By 21 September the encirclement of the city was complete, its inhabitants prisoners (less the Empress Eugénie, who with the aid of her American dentist and by dint of masquerading as a patient destined for a lunatic asylum had escaped the vengeance of the mob).

For the next four months, the siege of Paris mesmerized the

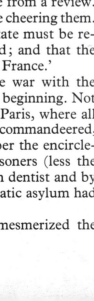

1870: a German troop train blown up by the French near Megieves in the early stages of the Franco-Prussian war.

world: every detail of resistance, of suffering, of diet, disease and death was eagerly consumed over the breakfast table, and helped, incidentally, to sway a great deal of public opinion away from the barbarous Prussian. The fact that these details were even available for publication abroad was a tribute to the ingenuity of the besieged; for amongst the hare-brained schemes put up to Paris's *Comité Scientifique* in those desperate days (including the magical 'decomposition' of air around the German encampments, and the forging of a titanic hammer to bash them on the head) one idea caught the public imagination.

This was balloons, a form of transport pioneered in France by the Montgolfier brothers but only now used to its greatest effect. Within two days of the siege, an indomitable 'aerostat', M. Durouf, made a successful flight from Montmartre to Evreux; after which an average of two or three a week rose into the outside world, carrying official despatches, news reports and private letters (at an inflated price, naturally). Most of them evaded the enemy guns and avoided landing in German-held territory; some of them travelled embarrassingly far, like the one which landed mystifyingly in the middle of Norway. The most sensational flight of the whole siege was that of Gambetta, the nation's most eloquent citizen. His mission was to raise an army from the provinces, who so far had shown themselves disappointingly unmoved by the fate of Paris. At first apprehensive,

Above: Before the 'impregnable' fortress of Sedan – a photograph taken on the very day of the French capitulation, 2 September 1870.

Right: Gambetta prepares to embark on his historic escape from the city, during the siege of Paris: Place St Pierre, Montmartre on 7 October 1870. His mission – to reach Tours and raise a relief army from the provinces.

German troops in possession
of Fort Issy, a strategic
defence-point of Paris, a
few days after the surrender
of the city and signing of
the armistice on 28 January,
1871. Inset: The Hall of
Mirrors in the Palace of
Versailles transformed into
a German military hospital.

Gambetta afterwards declared himself 'stunned with the overpowering idea of Nature's force and man's weakness', but admitted he had thanked heaven when he touched earth again 'where man has a *point de résistance* in struggling against the tyranny of creation.'

His historic flight took place on 7 October. Three weeks later his crusade took on a special urgency when it was learned that Metz had capitulated, with three marshals of France, over 6,000 officers and 173,000 men. In Paris Bazaine's surrender was regarded as an overwhelming act of treason, nor was French opinion mollified by reports such as appeared in the *Daily News*, from a correspondent who walked into the besieged town with the German army: 'I dined here this evening at the *table d'hôte* for 7 francs, including half a bottle of wine . . . We had four courses for dinner, and no horse-flesh – at least the waiter said not.'

Conditions were to get infinitely worse than that in the capital before any such defeatism was heard. On Christmas Eve, after three months of siege, a correspondent sent off a despatch to the *Daily News*: 'For food, there is little else left but bread and horse. Now and then we make a haul of something rich and rare. We had three enormous salmon the other day – at least they were called salmon; but I am not ichthyologist enough to say what they were . . . A few days ago, in the same first-rate restaurant in which I saw the supposed salmon, I was offered lamb for dinner. The proprietor declared most solemnly it was innocent lamb. What do you think it was? It was the opposite of lamb – it was wolf.' He was privileged indeed, compared with the ordinary inhabitant of the city, who had long since been grateful for a morsel of cat, rat, dog or sparrow. Even the zoo was unceremoniously raided, camels, kangaroos and the baby elephants Castor and Pollux falling to the demands of the human stomach (these last only the French genius for sauces could, apparently, make palatable). But the pigeons escaped, since they were daily doing their bit, carrying Nadar's amazing 'micro-photos' out of the city.

Yet for all its improvisations Paris was doomed, in spite of Gambetta's prodigious efforts in raising a provincial army 180,000-strong, in spite of a brave sortie *en masse* out of the beleaguered city to try and join him, and in spite of some impudent guerrilla raids by the old Italian patriot Garibaldi (to pay off his debt for French assistance during the Risorgimento). On 27 December, the bombardment of Paris began. 'They have burst upon the gardens of the Luxembourg, upon the Invalides, upon the Observatory, upon the boulevard and street which take their name from the hottest of all hot places – the Boulevard d'Enfer,' reported the *Daily News*. 'But most of all they seem to converge upon the Pantheon, for it appears that the Prussians have an idea that here is a powder magazine. There is not a grain of powder in the Pantheon – only hundreds of women and scores of men praying to Sainte Geneviève to save Paris.' In fact the German

From one cradle of liberty to another: republican France's gift to republican America, the Statue of Liberty, towers above the rooftops of Paris awaiting its shipment across the Atlantic (see page 100).

52

missiles caused little real damage and few casualties, being filled only with black powder. In that respect, as the correspondent said, it might just have well been a 'salvo of champagne bottles', but the real damage was to morale. This, combined with the increasing infant mortality due to hunger, with a worrying increase in disease, with the diminishing hopes of salvation from outside and, above all, with the 'siege fever' which was rapidly undermining Trochu's military government, helped to persuade Jules Favre that 'civil war was a few yards away.'

On 24 January Favre appeared in the German headquarters at Versailles, enquiring for Count Bismarck. His tears failed to move the Iron Chancellor to anything more than symbolic concession – like allowing the besieged to fire 'the last shot'. Bismarck, in his turn, insisted on a much more important symbol of conquest: the marching of his troops through Paris, past the Arc de Triomphe and down the Champs Elysées. And on 1 March, the day the French Assembly ratified the treaty of peace, they did so – as smartly as ever, but for the most part discreetly, through a city shrouded in mourning.

Even if history is a continuous narrative, now and then it can be conveniently paragraphed, and if the events of 1870–71 occasioned in Britain only mild astonishment, rather than a profound sense of shock, perspective allows us to regard those months as something of a landmark in the affairs of Europe. The real triumph of Chancellor Bismarck was not the humbling of France – no one appreciated better than he that the plunder of Alsace and Lorraine would rankle in France until it was revenged (as ultimately it was) – but in the emotional ceremony that took place in the Hall of Mirrors at Versailles one snowy morning in January 1871. There, beneath the tangible reminders of Louis XIV's great empire, the assorted dukes, grand dukes, princes and kings of a once-disunited Germany were assembled to hail the inauguration of the Second Reich and to crown William I of Prussia as its Emperor.

He had carried William on his shoulders to the Imperial throne, claimed Bismarck, with truth (if not with modesty). It had been, as he had promised, a process of 'blood and iron' strewn with the wreckage of Danish aspirations, Austrian pride and now French arrogance. Ten years ago, Germany had been a collection of thirty-eight independent states; now the military achievements of Prussia had welded them into a unified empire, foremost among the continental powers. After the Franco-Prussian war Bismarck declared Germany's expansion satiated: he knew where to stop and how not to give irreparable offence, so that the remainder of his long career was dedicated to maintaining an acceptable balance of power without – like a juggler keeping half a dozen plates in the air at once, the contemporary analogy went – and at the same time to extinguishing any signs of fragmentation within. This policy at home led him variously to lean on conservative Catholics through an alliance with the liberals (so that in 1876 you would have looked in vain for a Prussian bishop not in prison or in exile), then later – after a reconciliation with the Pope – on liberals and socialists with the aid of the Catholic Centre Party. Such contortions never struck him for one moment as bizarre, if the objective was the preservation of the State.

If the State that he had moulded proved to be an ambitious, militaristic monster, it was not a problem that exercised the Chancellor unduly, knowing that as long as Kaiser William I lived (and he lived to see 90) these ambitions could be held in check. On this simple soldierly man, 'a great plodder' as *The Times* patronisingly described him, such grandiose titles as 'All-Highest' denoted only a mark of respect. It was when they devolved on his unstable, melodramatic grandson that they assumed a new and ominous meaning, so that the court circular could in all seriousness publish the fact of the Kaiser's visit to church one Sunday as 'this morning the All-Highest went to pay his respects to the Highest.'

Nevertheless, the flame of German nationalism in the 1870s, kindled by the successes of the previous decade and in no way dampened by the writings of Treitschke or the operas of Wagner, burned fiercely in the breasts of the new generation. They watched Berlin being transformed into a monument to armed victory, the open drains making way to platz-fuls of belligerent statues and triumphant columns. They observed the growing fame of their scholars and scientists – of Schliemann at the site of Troy and Koch in pursuit of bacteria, of Daimler and his petrol engine, von Bunsen and his burner, and of Siemans, who exhibited an electric railway in Berlin as early as 1879. They marked the phenomenal growth of technology and capital, which between them were transforming vast areas of the Ruhr into industrial wastelands but, more important, were beginning to challenge the complacent monopolists of Britain. In the three years after the end of the war, as many blast-furnaces, iron-works and machine factories were built as had risen in the whole of the century so far. In one year alone, Alfred Krupp acquired more than 300 iron-ore mines, two new iron-works and a fleet of transport ships – and still have enough loose change to build himself a funereal 200-room mansion outside Essen.

As tasteless a memorial to mammon as the wit of man could devise ('an opera-house to which a railway station has been attached'), Krupp's castle was a symptom of a disturbing new contagion in Germany, a tendency to self-worship. Foreigners began to remark on this change. Where was the romanticism, the idealism of thirty years ago? 'Today, young idealist,' explained Charles Waldstein in the *Nineteenth Century*, attempting to analyse this new teutonic

Above: Rack-and-pinion mountain railway in the Alps, *c.* 1870. Right: Krupps' huge armament factory at Essen in 1880, a vital ingredient in Bismarck's policy of 'blood and iron'.

character, 'you must be a business man and make money, and wear a new coat and your hair short like everyone else, or you will be laughed at. This kills the very idealism which he needs: he finds all romance ridiculed.' Education attended to the intellect, he noted, but neglected the character, and a creeping conformity was everywhere to be seen. Above all, it had become an obsessively masculine society, where the young women were impressed with the Germanic virtues of 'church, children and cooking' and the young men played at duelling.

Mark Twain, who observed a number of bouts of duelling at Heidelberg University, doubted there was much play-acting about them. The young men wore goggles and padded the body, but their faces were entirely exposed – indeed the whole point was to obtain honourable scars, the more livid the better. 'Scars are plenty enough in Germany among the young men,' he wrote[36], 'and very grim ones they are, too. They criss-cross the face in angry red welts, and are permanent and ineffaceable. Some of these scars are of a very strange and dreadful aspect; and the effect is striking when several such accent the milder ones, which form a city map on a man's face.'

Symbolic freedom from tyranny: the tearing down of Napoleon I's statue by order of the Commune, 16 May 1871.

But in the aftermath of the war, scars were not the exclusive prerogative of German student corps. No Prussian blade in his gymnasium ever inflicted such wounds on his fellow-cadet as fellow-Frenchmen perpetrated on each other in the passions of the Commune, which raised its red banner over Paris on 18 March 1871. That day, Paris presented a sorry comparison with the gay city of Berlin (at that moment welcoming its new Emperor). The statue of Strasbourg was draped in black mourning, the gaping shell-holes around the Pantheon stood unrepaired almost unnoticed, an air of desolation overhung the city like a shroud. Up in Montmartre a detachment of soldiers sat idly around the cannon which the new government had ordered them to remove for the public safety, waiting for the horses and tackle they had omitted to bring with them.

Suddenly there was a mob around them, hurling abuse, defying them to remove the guns 'which had been made in Paris and belonged to Paris'. Weeks of tension which had fermented in the capital were beginning to explode into open confrontation between the citizens of Paris and the newly-elected government. Such was the fury of the growing multitude in Montmartre that the army – seeing no glory in defending a few lumps of iron – prudently melted away, though not before two senior officers had been murdered. The mayor of the district found himself powerless to prevent bloodshed: 'All were shrieking like wild beasts without realising what they were doing. I observed then that pathological phenomenon which might be called blood lust. A breath of madness seemed to have passed over this mob.' He was seen to have broken down when informed of the

murders. His name was Clemenceau, and the next time he was known to have broken down was in 1918 after the signing of the Armistice.

By evening, all the government troops had been pulled back to Versailles, and Paris's National Guard was to be found lounging outside the Hôtel de Ville, where within a slightly bemused group of revolutionaries – the *Comité Central* – found themselves the unexpected masters of the city. Paris had always boasted a long revolutionary tradition, time and again setting it at odds with the provinces, although rarely had the disillusion and bitterness run so deep as now. Parisians felt, with some reason, that they had borne the brunt of war and suffered the humiliation of occupation: it was they who had declared a republic and starved for its sake. Now what should they find, but that after the national elections in February more than four hundred representatives to the Assembly (assembled first in Bordeaux, then transferred to Versailles) were dedicated to the restoration of a monarchy – and the 43 radical voices of Paris were swamped by a deluge of country bumpkins. What had they been fighting for, they wondered.

After a week of confused argument in the Hôtel de Ville, the *Comité Central* informed them: an independant municipal council of Paris (or Commune), which would pave the way for such com-

Overleaf: National Guard and other heroes of the Commune parade for the camera at the foot of the Vendôme column (1871).

munes throughout France. The idea was not to fractionalize the country, rather to unite it – as a republic – into a federation of democracies, as the manifesto of the Commune explained:

The autonomy of the Commune will have as its only limit the right of autonomy equally valid for all other Communes. They are deceived or deceive the country who accuse Paris of aiming at the destruction of the French unity accomplished by the Revolution. . . . Political unity as Paris desires it, is the voluntary association of all local initiatives.

Marx, comfortably ensconced in Hampstead, might have viewed this socialist experiment with absorbing interest and hailed it as the overture to a drama which would sweep the world, but nearer to hand in Versailles the head of government was less convinced of that. Adolphe Thiers, however much of a firebrand he might have been once in his long career, was now in his old age a settled constitutionalist, and had no intention of allowing a fractious committee to destroy France. Summoning, with German consent, 100,000 prisoners-of-war back from the Fatherland, he laid seige to the city for the second time. It was necessarily to be a full-scale investment, heralded at the end of April by a remorseless barrage on outlying areas like Neuilly, where an English ambulanceman, Colonel John Stanley, arrived to find a desolate scene: 'I entered what had been beautiful houses, with floors wobbling and held up only by a side, utterly wrecked, billiard tables, looking-glasses, sofas and costly furniture all smashed to pieces, guns placed in lovely gardens, the walls broken through to enable them to pass from one garden to another . . . In many houses we found the dead laid out, where they had been placed some days ago, and the people had lived as they could in the cellars all this long time on bread and nothing else.'

Resistance in the capital itself was hampered by persistant quarrels among the communards, for ever shuffling military command from one leader to another, without any noticeable improvement in discipline. For a moment, in the second week of May, the emergence of Delescluze put some backbone into the National Guard, and on 16 May a morale-boosting ceremony took place in the Place Vendôme, where Napoleon I's 850-foot column was ritually demolished before 10,000 people and massed bands. The old Emperor proved rather more truculent than the engineers had bargained for, but in due course the monument fell 'on a heap of sand faggots prepared for it, with a mighty crash . . . the Column broke up almost before it reached its bed, and lay on the ground a huge mass of ruin,' described Colonel Stanley. 'An instant after a crowd of men, National Guards, Commune, and sight-seeing English flew upon it, and commenced to get bits of it as remembrance, but the excitement was so intense that people moved about as in a dream.'

It was a futile gesture. Thiers and his army now stood uncom-

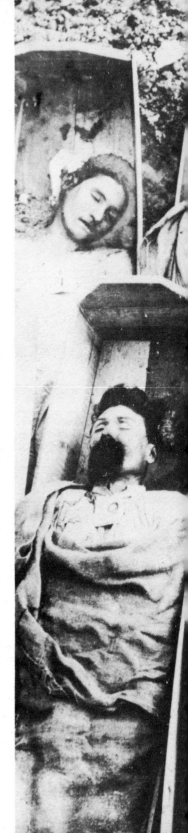

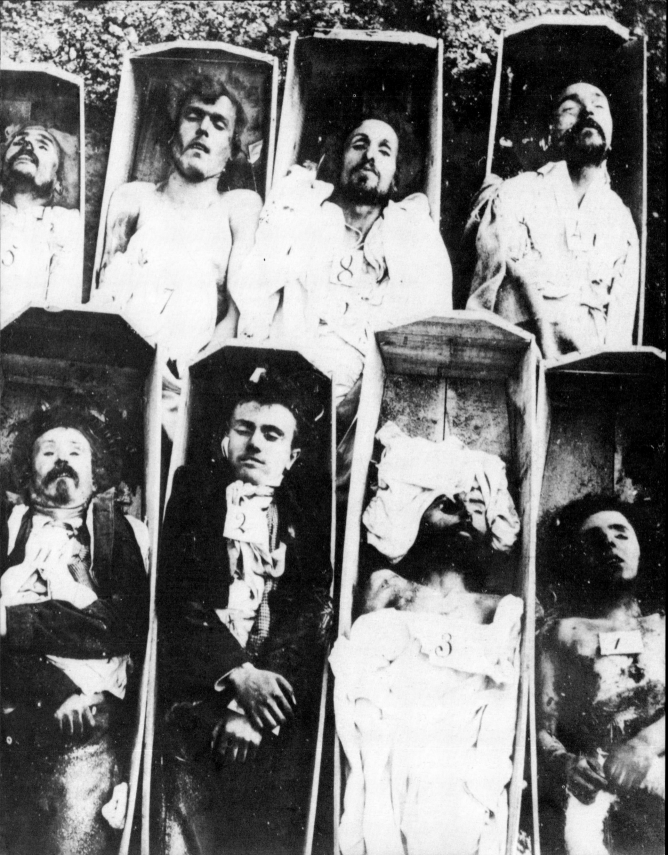

promisingly in the very suburbs. On 21 May they entered Paris through a gate pounded into rubble and left unguarded: the carnage began. Behind their formidable barricades of omnibuses, sand-bags and paving-stones, the communards fought with the ferocity of despair, yielding only one street for yet another. For a week the invasion went on, compounding unspeakable atrocities on both sides: the arbitrary slaughter of the Commune's hostages (including the Archbishop of Paris), and in turn the senseless butchery of captured insurgents. It was enough for a man to display blackened hands to condemn him as a sniper, for a woman to be carrying a bottle to mark her as a *pétroleuse* – one of those shadowy agents said to be systematically firing the city.

All over Paris conflagrations raged, engulfing the Hôtel de Ville and the Tuileries – and by only a miracle sparing the Louvre. By 28 May only a handful of fanatics in the 20th *arondissement* were holding out, resigned to death. Two months after its official proclamation the Commune officially died, but the killing continued with unreasoning reprisals, feuds, denunciations. At the barricades, or later in prison basements, Paris lost 25,000 lives in those ten days – and its good name as a citadel of civilization.

The Commune and its terrible extinction bequeathed a long legacy of bitterness, yet Paris recovered with unquenchable optimism – as did the Republic, for in spite of the overwhelming monarchist inclinations of the Assembly it could not decide from which hereditary branch a king should be found, the House of Orléans or that of Bourbon. The likeliest claimant, the Comte de Chambord (a Bourbon), was exhumed from his comfortable Viennese estates and found to be an immutable aristocrat of the old school with an aversion to the tricolor. His terms, coming so soon after the Commune, proved to be totally unrealistic and he returned quite content to Austria. Napoleon was by now dead, and the Orleanist Comte de Paris, having already admitted Chambord's claim, crumbled before the rhetoric of Gambetta and his republicans – who between 1873 and 1875 actually gained twenty-six new supporters in the Assembly out of twenty-nine by-elections. France, after all, didn't seem to be doing too badly under a republic: the Germans had quit French soil within two years, and the 'crippling' indemnity had been paid off with astonishing ease. So that when the question of formalizing the republic came up in 1875, it was actually sanctioned – albeit by a single vote. Henry James was in Paris in 1876 (as a columnist for the *New York Tribune*) and observed those hectic months as a brand-new Senate and Chamber were elected and the National Assembly passed into history. 'By hook and by crook, through thick and thin,' he told his American readers[19], 'by something that seemed at times like a clumsy accident, the Republic has been weaned from babyhood and set on its feet. There are plenty of people who promise you it can't walk alone – that

64

it will tumble over and crack its pate. But . . . the wisest of doctors and nurses declare that if it is given the chance it will toddle; and now fortunately every year its legs are growing longer.'

James noted also that the tourists were beginning to flock back to the pleasure-capital of Europe, harbingered as usual by the British: 'You recognise him [the British tourist] farther off than you do an American; he makes a more vivid spot in the picture. He is always and everywhere the same – carrying with him, in his costume and physiognomy, that indefinable expression of not considering anything out of England worth making, physically or morally, a toilet for.' If these scruffy, under-dressed trippers had spent their time doing more than window-shopping, they would have discovered that Paris was recovering some of its pre-war *joie de vivre*. Not the unbridled extravagances of the Empire perhaps, but the *cafés chantants* had survived – like the Eldorado and the Folies-Bergère – the *Bals* (pleasure-gardens) were as splendid as ever, and the carriages in the Bois de Boulogne as elegant. Evenings at the Odéon, the Comédie Française, the Opéra were illuminated by the plays of Dumas, the acting of Sarah Bernhardt, the music of Delibes. True, a cloud had settled over the literary world in 1876 with the death of George Sand, but at Flaubert's Sunday afternoons you could meet Zola, de Goncourt and Maupassant. Nor had the French lost their flair for

Vienna in 1881, on the occasion of the wedding of the Emperor's son, Rudolph, to the Belgian princess, Stephanie. Eight years later the Crown Prince was to shoot himself – supposedly because of his father's opposition to a divorce from Stephanie.

Cultural colossi: Sarah
Bernhardt (above), toast
of the Comédie Française
in the 1870s, and Claude
Monet (left) in his *atelier*.

expositions – *concours, carrousels, salons* and *palais* of all kinds – and plans were well under way for a grand Universal Exhibition in 1878 which would rival even Napoleon's World Fair.

As an art critic, James visited and re-visited the Salon describing its exhibits in detail, but the names of its luminaries – whom he so much admired – fall on our ears today with a dull thud of unrecognition after nearly a century of acquaintance with the Impressionists. Yet it was only as an afterthought that he took himself off to Durand-Ruel's gallery to see for himself the second exhibition by this clique (in which Degas, Monet and Renoir were well represented but which *Le Figaro* called 'a frightening spectacle of human vanity gone astray to the point of madness'). Henry James was less opinionated, but cool:

An exhibition for which I may at least claim that it can give rise to no dangerous perversities of taste is that of the little group of the Irreconcilables – otherwise known as the 'Impressionists' in painting . . . and I have found it decidedly interesting. But the effect of it was to make me think better than ever of all the good rules which decree that beauty is beauty and ugliness ugliness, and warn us off from the sophistications of satiety . . . These young contributors to the exhibition are partisans of unadorned reality and absolute foes to arrangement, embellishment, selection, to the artist's allowing himself . . . to be preoccupied with the idea of the beautiful. None of its members show signs of possessing first-rate talent, and indeed the 'Impressionist' doctrines strike me as incompatible, in an artist's mind, with the existence of first-rate talent.

Above: The Galérie des Machines at Paris's Universal Exhibition of 1878 proved to the world at large that France had been battered but not bowed by the events of 1870/71.

68

It was a point of view many of his contemporaries would have found faultless, but which James at least had the grace to disavow later.

The English journalist, George Augustus Sala, visiting Paris in 1878 for the Exhibition and again two years later 'in search of sunshine'[25], pronounced the city completely convalescent if not actually regenerate, happily reporting that 'at no time during my acquaintance with Paris have the shop-windows presented such an astounding exhibition of pictorial and plastic, but chiefly photographic indecency, as they do at the present moment.' Moving nearer the sun, to the South of France, he found the Riviera vulgarly prosperous from its annual winter influx of Englishmen. Even before Queen Victoria set her gracious seal of approval on the area (in 1882) they acted as if they had discovered the place – which they had, really. Biarritz and the Pyrenean spas, too, were profiting from the decline of the once-fashionable German watering-places (where no patriotic Frenchman would anyway set foot).

But wherever in France you might have gone in the 1870s, one spectre of disaster was never far away. Phylloxera was a beetling bug which was laying waste the entire vineyards of France (the only consolation being that it was beetling slowly through the Rhineland as well). This plague, brought in on imported American vines, had been first noticed in the sixties; in the next decade it brought ruin to Burgundy and Cognac (where two-thirds of the vines were never replanted) and many lesser areas. At first it looked as if the great clarets of Bordeaux might be spared – producing in the 1870s a particularly fine series of vintages – but phylloxera was an indiscriminate gourmand and struck there as well.

For many countrymen it brought immense hardship. Robert Louis Stevenson, travelling through Languedoc on a donkey[28], came upon a rare sight in those parts. 'One thing more I note. The phylloxera has ravaged the vineyards in this neighbourhood, and in the early morning, under some chestnuts by the river, I found a party of men working with a cider-press. I could not at first make out what they were after, and asked a fellow to explain. "Making cider," he said. *"Oui, c'est comme ça. Comme dans le nord!"* There was a ring of sarcasm in his voice: the country was going to the devil.'

Nor could Gallic ingenuity come up with an answer to start with, nor an acceptable substitute. In another region Stevenson travelled through, 'the phylloxera was in the neighbourhood; and instead of wine we drank at dinner a more economical juice of the grape – *La Parisienne*, they call it. It is made by putting the fruit whole into a cask with water; one by one the berries ferment and burst; what is drunk during the day is supplied at night in water. So with ever another pitcher from the well and ever another grape exploding and giving its strength, one cask of Parisienne may last a family till spring. It is, as the reader will anticipate, a feeble beverage . . .' In due course,

Overleaf: Ancient democracy in ruins – how tourists in the 1870s saw the Erechtheum, on the Acropolis in Athens. It took another thirty years for this marvel of antiquity to be restored.

to the relief of France (and the world) it was discovered that the answer lay in grafting on resistant American vines. A repayment by the New World to the Old, of which James would heartily have approved.

From the South of France Sala made his way – still hopefully in search of sun – to Venice and on to Rome. Both cities had changed almost beyond recognition since they had been joyfully incorporated into the new united kingdom of Italy. With his amazing ubiquity he had happened to be in both places on the days they had won their 'liberation' – Venice at the conclusion of the Austro-Prussian war in 1866, and Rome in the early days of the Franco-Prussian war in 1870. He had watched the Austrian garrison in the gold-embroidered uniforms sail away down the Grand Canal for the last time, while 'the ladies of the Venetian nobility, who for years had worn nothing but funereal sables, sat in low-necked ball-dresses . . . to the clangour of trumpets, the roar of artillery and the shouts of a hundred thousand people.' On that memorable day the old grey palaces had been festooned with tapestries, carpets, silks and satins, and the frontage of St Marks had been hidden by a mass of Italian flags. Now, fifteen years later, he was bound to admit Venice was depressing, its canals profaned by 'puffing, gasping and clattering twopenny steamers', its flower-girls turned into importunate slatterns, its Tintoretto hues dulled. He put it down to the lack of sun, and moved on.

Rome was altogether a different matter. In 1870, it had stood out like a wart on the honeyed political skin of Italy, the personal property (together with the Papal States) of a Pope who had just proclaimed himself dogmatically infallible, but whose temporal power was only propped up by the good offices of Napoleon III and his resident Zouaves. It was the last stronghold to hold out against Italian nationalism which under Cavour, Garibaldi and Victor Emmanuel had triumphed in the sixties from Sicily to Savoy. Rome's fall was unexpected and almost bloodless: in September 1870, the French regiments were withdrawn to Paris to help stem the advancing German tide. Once again, Sala was there, following the Italian army which 'knocked down a few stone walls and overcame a few gallant Papal zouaves on their march to the Quirinal.' But then came the deluge:

Every train seemed to be laden, not only with piles of Milanese, Genoese and Florentine newspapers, hitherto inaccessible to Romans of liberal opinions . . . but also with enterprising gentlemen of advanced political views, who as soon as ever they had deposited their carpetbag at an hotel, proceeded to organise, edit, and to publish brand-new newspapers for themselves. . . . Hitherto unheard-of hairdressers hung up their signboards at street corners, quite unexpectedly. A strange man from Turin suddenly proclaimed that he had twenty thousand pairs of ladies' and gentlemen's boots to dispose of for ready money at surprisingly low prices. And from under the very lees of venerable monasteries and austere theological seminaries new cafés and new restaurants made an unblushing appearance; while – scandal upon scandal – coquettishly-attired young females of alluring mien, and bearing trim little baskets full of flowers tripped saucily from café to café, accosting gentlemen to whom they had never been introduced, and in the coolest manner imaginable sticking posies into the stranger's button-hole.

Gone now from the streets were the monks and friars begging for alms, and the gilded coaches of the cardinals – and the once-familiar Antibes Legion were as much a part of history as Attila's Huns. Returning at the end of the decade to see what had taken their place, Sala found tramway cars, no less, and a spanking new Via Nazionale running from the Baths of Diocletian to the Forum: he found an earnest Roman Season in full swing, with much importing of upright pianos into hotel suites and 'five o'clock tea' very fashionable for the Du Maurier matrons, who now discovered they approved of the New Rome. On the other hand, there were some who categorically did not, like Mrs Hugh Fraser, an American girl living in Rome, whose later marriage to an English diplomat took her all around the world[15]. She looked upon the fall of Rome as the unhappiest two weeks of her life: though only a 'Catholic at heart', she professed unbounded admiration for Pope Pius IX and rejoiced in the decorous social life that had flourished under his aegis, even as 'hordes of Garibaldians

Picnic and porterage up Mount Vesuvius in 1880.

and Mazzinists were constantly stirring up revolution'. She regarded the advent of a new era with very different eye to the worldly old Sala, believing that the men of the conquering army, 'good Catholics from decent parishes all over the north, hated the job and expected condign punishment from Heaven for the sacrilege they had been forced to commit'; while 'the socialist, the revolutionist, the atheist, the men who had been shunned by all decent people . . . could call the Holy Father by villainous names with all impunity now. When Porta Pia was battered down a tide of prostitutes flowed in on the city; disorderly houses sprang up like weeds in the night; indecent pictures and obscene literature were flaunted in the streets.'

Her return to Rome a few years later, unlike Sala's, simply convinced her that Rome had been desecrated beyond recovery, and she was relieved when her husband was posted to Vienna where civilized society was more settled. It was not just settled, she discovered when she arrived, it was ossified. No one, but no one outside *the* four hundred noble families (and the diplomatic corps) could hope to knock on the portals for admittance to Austrian society '. . . which for minute etiquette and delicate gradations cannot be matched in the world,' as Mrs Fraser put it. Anyone not bred to its rigours might have found upper-class life under the Habsburgs shatteringly boring or else suffocatingly comfortable. Yet, from without, it was still regarded with envy: musical soirées presided over by the Strauss family

Above: The superior way to travel for visitors to Madeira in 1880. Right: The perilous way for intrepid ramblers across the Mer de Glace at Chamonix, 1885.

(Edward and Josef, for the most part), coffee and bonbons at Sacher's, the Riding School, and glittering nights at the Opera or Ring Theatre (before it burned down just before curtain-up one evening, with hundreds of spectators tragically still trapped inside). And then the obligatory, exclusive Court balls and receptions, during which the mettlesome Empress Elizabeth 'took very little trouble to hide the weariness and distaste which the obligation involved', and over which she very often presided by proxy.

The Emperor Franz Joseph, too, had little time for the frivolities, applying himself fourteen hours a day to an undiminishing pile of paperwork and training his household staff to serve and clear a twelve-course meal in under an hour. In spite of two crushing defeats in ten years (in Italy, 1859 and against the Prussians at Koniggratz, 1866) his army, with its theatrical and quite impracticable uniforms, remained the light of his life and few things pleased him more than a swanky military review of soldiers who never won a war. No human being could have kept his finger on the pulse of an Empire which comprised twelve separate nationalities and which stretched from Germany to the Iron Gates, from Russia to Italy, whose nationalist tensions were mutually contradictory and whose political institutions were complex beyond the dreams of metaphysics. By the 1870s it was officially a Dual Monarchy, whereby the empire of Austria and the

kingdom of Hungary were linked in the person of Franz Joseph (as a result of the 'settlement' of 1867, which aimed at appeasing the age-old problem of Magyar nationalism), and if such legalistic convolutions did not make for an efficient state, it did at least survive for the remainder of Franz Joseph's generous life-span.

For the Emperor, in a paternal kind of way, was affectionately regarded by his people. Mrs Fraser recalled watching the traditional ceremony of the Washing of the Feet on Holy Thursday, a ritual relic perhaps of the once Holy Roman Empire which partly summed up the whole benevolent despotism of the Habsburgs. 'Then the guests were brought in, the oldest poor men and women in Vienna, twelve of each, certified to be respectable and needy. . . The guests' foot-gear having been already removed by their friends, the Sovereigns went down on their knees and washed the old feet devoutly, the ewers and towels being held for them by Archdukes and Archduchesses. As the Emperor went down the line he chatted and laughed with the aged men, and the expression of rapturous joy and humility was worth going far to see.' And it was also, she thought, a salutary reminder that beneath the gloss – the waltzes and beer-cellars and *Volks-gartens* – there was a less endearing side to the Empire: the appalling poverty of millions, whom the economic depression of the late seventies drove in their hundreds of thousands to seek a new life across the Atlantic; the rigid class structures, which buttressed privilege and encouraged apathy to a degree unparalleled anywhere in Europe; and the sinister undercurrent of anti-semitism (which surfaced with tragic results fifty years later). 'The Rothschilds were, for instance, abominably treated by them,' remarked Mrs Fraser, 'although they were pleasant unassuming people who never got in anybody's way. Of course the hatred of Jews had something to do with it, but considering that there were very few families who had not been helped at one time or another by Jew money, the thing in this case seemed unjust.'

One anomaly, above all, Mrs Fraser could not find it in her heart to forgive.

After dinner the usual shock to one's artistic appreciations was administered when eighteen or twenty charming, refined young women trooped into the smoking-room, selected large, strong cigars and stuck them into their pretty mouths. . . . There is no suggestion of roughness or rowdiness in the sight of dainty ladies, who know how to do it taking a few whiffs of a delicate cigarette – also the calming digestive effect of the little smoke is particularly beneficial to women – but the cigar is an abomination, and during all my stay in Vienna I could never get over the repulsion inspired by the sight of it in a feminine mouth, especially when the delinquent was in full evening dress, covered with jewels, wearing hothouse flowers, and looking – till the fatal moment – like a flower herself.

It was an irony of fate that Mr Fraser's next posting was in Peking. She does not comment on the smoking that went on *there*.

The Ottoman Empire & Russia: Absolute Enemies

The Golden Horn, Constantinople.

Then, in 1875, events took a turn in south-east Europe which once more directed men's attention – a slightly tired attention, for it was an old story – to the ramshackle empire of the Ottomans. The Turkish dynasty, once unarguably the greatest in the world, was now in its dotage. It still stretched from Egypt to the frontiers of Austria–Hungary and deep into Asia, but the crushing weight of its corrupt government and antedeluvian economy had earned it the all-too-appropriate sub-title of 'sick man of Europe'. Like other world-weary and decadent empires it still presented an intriguing facade. Mark Twain, who had visited Constantinople a few years earlier[34], found it made a noble picture: 'Seen from the anchorage, it is by far the handsomest city we have seen. Its dense array of houses swells upwards from the water's edge, and spreads over the domes of many hills: and the gardens that peep out here and there, the great globes of the mosques, and the countless minarets that meet the eye every-where invest the metropolis with the quaint Oriental aspect one dreams of when he reads of eastern travel.'

But its appeal began and ended with the picturesque. In reality it was 'an eternal circus. People were thicker than bees, in those narrow streets, and the men were dressed in all the outrageous, outlandish, idolatrous, extravagant, thunder-and-lightning costumes that ever a tailor with the delirium tremens and seven devils could conceive of.' He gazed askance at the closets they called shops with Turks sitting cross-legged on the threshold, smoking long pipes and smelling 'like Turks. That covers the ground.' He stared at the goose-ranchers, driving a hundred geese before them in the hope of selling a few. He disapproved of Santa Sophia ('the rustiest old barn in heathendom'), and gaped at the Dancing Dervishes ('about as barbarous an exhibition as we have witnessed'). Of the beggars: 'If you want dwarfs – I mean just a few dwarfs for a curiosity – go to Genoa. If you wish to buy them by the gross, for retail, go to Milan. But if you would see the very heart and home of cripples and human monsters, both, go straight to Constantinople.'

Much of this was, inevitably, in the eye of the beholder. William Howard Russell, accompanying the Prince of Wales on a state visit[24], observed a more glamorous side. He approved the 'gas in all the main streets on both sides of the Golden Horn, and the abundant water supply', though he was rather more dubious about the disappearance of 'the grand old turban – moolahs and fanatics are the only people who wear them; the fez in all its ugliness is the universal substitute.' He noticed too that 'the women have discarded the great yellow pooshes or slipper, and toddle about in patent leather spring boots of the newest Frankish fashion; but they still retain the most charm-ing of all dresses, though we hear that crinolines are not unknown beneath these flowing robes of silk!' Not that the ladies had advanced so far as to discard their yashmaks which, he thought, lent rather than detracted from the beauty of the face: 'Over this milk-white foil the black but rather bead-like eyes flash from under the straight painted eyebrows with no doubtful lustre or expression. Will fashion ever import this delicate lure into Europe?' he wondered, adding a little sourly, 'There can be no question of its efficacy in many cases which cannot be cured by the ordinary Paris *modistes*.'

A resident of the Middle East, James Baker, also noted a new sophistication in the seventies, especially among the women[3]: 'They are for the most part decked out in the latest Paris fashions, instead of the Turkish dress, and they delight to receive the visits of English and other foreign ladies – an innovation which a few years ago was of very rare occurrence. . . . In the streets of Constantinople the ladies of the harem may be seen driving about in their handsome broughams to do their shopping, and with their faces enveloped with so thin a yashmak that, like a slight cloud over the sun, it but tempers the brightness which lies behind.'

But even he discerned no change in the day-to-day transactions of Turkish administration. His efforts to acquire a passport were thwarted by officials whose 'principle duties appeared to consist in paring their nails and uttering deep and reflective sighs. There are', he added, 'usually three officials helping a fourth to do nothing.' Inertia was more than a way of life, it had been elevated to an art-form. 'The apathy and procrastination in every department of the State, great and small, in every private house, high and low, in every transaction, however important or however trifling, are the causes which attenuate progress to such meagre proportions. The Turkish official seldom refuses, but always postpones. If I had to devise a Turkish banner, I should inscribe on one side of it "*Evet, Effendim*" (certainly, sir), on the other "*Yarin*" (tomorrow), and below, the motto "There is but one God and backshish is His prophet".'

Presiding over his polyglot millions was the Sultan, Abdul Aziz, an ignorant and boorish individual, whose pastimes included releasing a crateful of chickens in the harem, then attempting to catch them. 'A man', declared Mark Twain, 'who found his great Empire a blot upon the earth – a degraded, poverty-stricken, miserable, infamous agglomeration of ignorance, crime and brutality, and will idle away the allotted days of his trivial life, and then pass to dust and the worms and leave it so.' In the summer of 1875, however, it began to look as if events were not going to wait upon his 'allotted days', when news started to filter through to the capital of a rebellion in the province of Bosnia.

For centuries the people of Bosnia (now the northern part of Yugoslavia) had lived in an uneasy state of racial and religious co-existence, the Christian Slav peasants with their Turkish Moslem overlords. There had been uprisings before, when poor harvests had made the farmers' tithe of one-third an intolerable burden, and these

Seat of the Sublime Porte
and the Achilles' heel of
Europe, Constantinople
and the Bosphorus, viewed
from the European side.

Overleaf: Russian Orthodox pilgrims at the river Jordan, near Jericho, receiving baptism from their own priests.

had duly been met with the familiar, refined cruelties of the Turkish regime – as the archaeologist Arthur Evans learned during his tour of the country in search of antiquities[11]:

A village will occasionally band together to defend themselves from these extortioners. Thereupon the tithe-farmer applies to the civil power, protesting that if he does not get the full amount from the village, he will be unable in his turn to pay the Government. The Zaptiehs, the factotums of the Turkish officials, are immediately quartered on the villagers and . . . with the aid of these gentry all kinds of personal tortures are applied to the recalcitrant. In the heat of summer men are stripped naked and tied to a tree smeared over with honey and left to the tender mercies of the insect world. A favourite plan is to drive a party of *rayahs* (peasants) up a tree or into a chamber, and then smoke them with green wood. Instances are recorded of Bosnian peasants being buried up to their heads in earth, and left to repent at leisure . . .

Evans was still in Bosnia when the 1875 revolt broke out, and quickly realized this was something more than the local disturbances of the past when he witnessed the long trains of refugees heading for the Austrian border and, even more ominous, the arrival of the dreaded Bashi-Bazouks, the Turkish irregulars whose animal ruthlessness was a byword throughout Europe. Not long ago they had been 'suppressed for conduct too outrageous for even the worst of governments to tolerate,' he explains, but once again they were streaming into Sarajevo, 'committing the wildest atrocities – cutting down women, children and old men who come in their way, and burning the crops and homesteads of the *rayah*.'

Prudently, Evans joined the flood of exiles and returned to London, as fresh sparks of insurrection ignited all over the Balkan provinces, Herzogovina, Montenegro, Serbia and Bulgaria. And with every new flashpoint the chancelleries of Europe took on a grimmer and more urgent aspect, reminding people once more that this backward and unpredictable corner of Europe was everyone's Achilles' heel: Moscow's, because she was there thwarted of a southern access for her navy; Vienna's, because of the ever-present contagion of Pan-Slav nationalism, which might infect her own volatile empire; Berlin's, because international conflict there would shatter Bismarck's fingertip balance of power in Europe; and London's, because any further weakening of Turkish sovereignty became an open invitation to Russian expansion.

At first, Disraeli was inclined to dismiss the more sensational reports of Balkan atrocities which now began to appear in the British press – 'coffee-house babble' he called it and put it down to Russian propaganda. But they continued to pour in over the wires, in particular from the correspondent of the *Daily News*, one Januarius Aloysius MacGahan, an American.

The atrocities admitted on all hands by those friendly to the Turks, and by the Turks themselves, are enough and more than enough. When you are met in the outset of your investigation with the admission that sixty or seventy villages have been

Moscow, 1870. Water-carts assemble at the fountain outside the China Gate. Inset: The eternal Kremlin skyline, from the east.

burned; that some 15,000 people have been slaughtered, of whom a large part were women and children, you begin to feel that it is useless to go any further. When in addition to this, you have horrid details of the violent outrages committed upon women, the hacking to pieces of helpless children, and spitting them upon bayonets; and when you have these details reported to you by the hundreds, not by the Bulgarians, but by the different consuls at Philippopolis and the German officials on the railway, as well as Greeks, Armenians, priests, missionaries and even Turks themselves, you begin to feel that any further investigation is superfluous.

His reports, the long columns of fund-raising appeals in *The Times* for unpronounceable towns full of *dz* and *nj*, then the full majesty of Gladstone weighing in with his shock-pamphlet *The Bulgarian Horrors* soon began to stir the public conscience. But by then circumstances in Constantinople itself had changed dramatically. In the summer of 1876, Abdul Aziz's government – which had already declared itself bankrupt – was toppled in a palace revolution by a secret society calling itself the Young Ottomans. Into his place stepped – or rather reeled – his nephew Murad, part lunatic and complete alcoholic, whom it was found judicious, after three months, to confine to his harem to make way for his brother Abdul Hamid. This morbid young man (who insisted on taking precautions for his personal safety far beyond the frontiers of neurosis) immediately displayed a duplicity remarkable even for an Osmanli, by granting a constitution with one hand and with his other dismissing the liberal premier, Midhat Pasha, the one man who could have rendered it anything more than a dead letter. Into this hiatus there arrived at the Sublime Porte, in March 1877, a 'protocol' from the Powers threatening intervention if the Sultan did not soon implement his promised reforms and ease the burdens of his Christian subjects. On 12 April Abdul Hamid refused the protocol. Twelve days later Russia, taking matters into her own hands, declared war.

Tsar Alexander II of Russia was a Romanov, and as such no less dedicated to his dynasty's sacred principles of absolute autocracy than his predecessors. Yet during the 1860s he had contrived to acquire a reputation for reform, with his emancipation of the serfs and the introduction of local government, which had spread far beyond his own boundaries. Indeed, when he came to visit Queen Victoria in 1874, *Punch* reported, he was very cordially received and fêted with fireworks. The magazine even composed a little ditty in his honour which must have sounded strange in the ears of a Tsar:

> *Freedom and Love, go forth to meet*
> *The Czar on Welcome's wings;*
> *Yours are the smiles the Guest to greet,*
> *Who such credentials brings.*

The credentials, it must be admitted, had been somewhat tarnished

by his fierce suppression of a revolt in Poland and there would have
been quite a few of his subjects, spied on and hounded by the sinister
secret police, who might have regarded that clarion-call of Freedom
as just a little hollow.

It availed Alexander nothing, in the end, that he had initiated
Russia's greatest piece of social legislation in the nineteenth century:
no less than three assassination attempts were made on him by revolutionaries. The third, in March 1881 – a bomb thrown by a Polish
student in the streets of St Petersburg – succeeded, and plunged
Russia back into the darkness of repression. Not that the 1870s were
any advertisement for enlightenment: the supposedly outlawed
knout and the prison camp were regularly inflicted upon members of
the extremist Will of the People movement, often called (somewhat
confusingly) nihilists – a term invented by Turgenev which seemed to
embrace every deviationist, from respectable idealists to the bomb-
apostles of Bakunin.

Colonel Wellesley, the British military attaché in Russia at this
time, recalled being invited to a nihilist dinner, much to his surprise[40].

I had expected to be taken mysteriously by my friend to some remote suburb where
nothing but squalor and crime were to be seen, whereas the dinner in reality took
place within a very short distance of the house in which I lived. My next cause of
astonishment were the appearance and demeanour of the men I had been invited to
meet. I do not mean I had expected to be introduced to shock-headed ruffians with
long hair and dirty sheepskin coats . . . but I was certainly not prepared to be received
by the quiet, plausible and moderate men with whom I sat down to dinner. . . . My
hosts were of the upper middle class and, with the exception of a few pardonable
outbursts against the existing form of Government and its ruthless methods, nothing
was said that was not based on common sense and logical argument.

Life in St Petersburg did not appeal to this officer: the long cold nights,
the appalling roads and back-breaking droshkies, the self-conscious
laziness of the people (which he attributed to the climate). But
'Curiously enough,' he noted, 'the minimum of political liberty and
the maximum of social freedom are to be found side by side under this
strange autocratic Government. Although in Russia the press is
gagged, obnoxious articles in foreign newspapers are obliterated, and
the native dares not even whisper an opinion as to politics, he can
have his supper at a restaurant at 1 a.m. if it so pleases him . . .'
Moscow was more to his taste, more 'thoroughly Russian' with its
Grand Opera, clean restaurants, open-air gymnasium ('lighted by
electric light for acrobatic performances'), bowling alleys and troupes
of café-dancers.

Wellesley, not being perhaps of a cultural bent, makes no mention
of Russia's remarkable literary flowering, which saw Tolstoy,
Dostoievsky, Goncharov, Turgenev all producing some of their
greatest works, nor of its impressive musical array – Tchaikovsky,
Borodin, Rimsky Korsakov, Moussorgsky. But his imagination was

Overleaf: Count Bismarck addressing the Congress of Berlin, 1878, an assembly of the European powers convened to 'settle' the Eastern Question and achieve, in the words of Disraeli, 'peace with honour'.

The funeral cortège of Czar Alexander II, at the spot where he was fatally wounded in St Petersburg by a Nihilist's bomb thrown into his carriage (1881).

caught by the seven-day wonders of the Black Sea, Admiral Popov's circular battleships, upon which the Government was lavishing vast sums of money. He was present in 1873 at the launching of the first of these rotund ironclads. 'Needless to say that Admiral Popov was the hero of the hour. The great vessel was launched head foremost from ways specially constructed so as not to injure any of her six crews. The successful launch of the ship was a signal for everyone to kiss everyone else, an operation which lasted a considerable time, and in which Admiral Popov was, of course, the most favoured.' The next day the ship was made to 'spin round like a teetotum on her own axis', a process which took precisely one minute and nineteen seconds, and caused 'Admiral Popov to be again embraced by his many admirers, male and female'.

If Wellesley had scant regard for the buffooneries of the Imperial navy, he had even less for the Russian army. He observed the mobilization in readiness for the march on Turkey, and had to admit he 'did not entirely agree with those who looked upon the defeat of the Turks as a certainty. On the contrary, I thought it not improbable that the Turks would be victorious. The same lack of initiative, the same

state of unpreparedness, the same general chaos were as apparent at the commencement of the Russo-Turkish War as they were at the beginning of the Crimean campaign in 1854.' Few in England, however, shared his view. Here the former indignation at Turkish brutishness melted as the Cossacks drew ever nearer to the Bosphorus – Kars, Plevna, Shipka Pass, Adrianople – and turned into a flood-tide of 'jingoist' war fever that found its voice in a ludicrous popular song:

> *We don't want to fight, but by jingo if we do,*
> *We've got the ships, we've got the men, we've got the money too!*

The Cabinet ordered the fleet to the Dardenelles . . . pulled it back . . . then sent it off again, in an agony of indecision. It made no difference anyway. Within nine months the Russians were camped outside the gates of Constantinople. The Sultan was beaten, and bloody had been his people's fall, especially where Serb and Bulgar had risen up in the van of the advancing Russians. Archibald Forbes vowed he would never forget the ghastly sights of that terrible march from Philippopolis to Adrianople[13].

Not a kilometre of it was there that did not lie among corpses, dead animals, broken arabas, piles of rags and straytatters of cast-off clothing. The two antagonistic races, Turk and Bulgarian, had found here an arena wherein to work off the blood-feuds of generations. There lay side by side the bodies of Bulgarian peasants with gaping wounds, often abominably mutilated, and side by side with those, corpses of dignified old Turks, their white beards clotted with blood, their hands closed on their bare chests. Between the races there had evidently been war to the knife . . . and children who had been frozen to death now lay in the snow as if still alive.

The treaty imposed on helpless Turkey at San Stefano, not surprisingly, was not at all to the taste of the other European powers, emasculating Turkey-in-Europe and creating a huge pro-Russian state of Bulgaria. After a certain amount of sabre-rattling and a rare show of unanimity between Britain and Austria, Russia was called to account at a congress in Berlin. In her isolation she had no practical alternative but to accept the revised terms of peace, which proved, if anything, that the pen was mightier than the sword. Eleven million Christians were indeed liberated from the Ottoman yoke, and the Tsar clung grimly on to his Asiatic conquests: but Austria, it was noted, obtained virtual control of Bosnia and Herzegovina, while Britain announced she had come by Cyprus under the new arrangements. Peace with honour, Disraeli proclaimed it, and no one denied that the prospect of a general European holocaust had been dispelled by statesmanship. But the loosening of the cords that bound the Tsar to his fellow-Emperors – which began under Bismarck's very nose, there in Berlin – was to lead the world tragically back, less than forty years later, to the place where this whole sorry episode had begun: Sarajevo.

North America: Distant Magnets

Promontory Point, Utah: 10 May 1869

At Promontory Point, in the salt and rock wilderness of Utah, one day in May 1869 a simple ceremony was performed. One end of a silver plate was bolted on to the Union Pacific railroad, the other on to the Central Pacific. The first great transcontinental railroad was complete (if you didn't count having to alight, bag and baggage, at Council Bluffs, Iowa, to cross the Missouri in a ferry), and in cities on both coasts the bells rang out to advertise the fact, and hymns ascended to heaven in thanks for this symbolic wedlock of East and West.

Among the lesser consequences of this great feat of engineering was the flood of tourists who flocked to find the elusive 'frontier' in comfort, and round-the-world travellers, who preferred this route to the hazards of Cape Horn. American Secretary of State William Henry Seward elected to begin his global wanderings on the Union Pacific in 1870, as did a London policeman's wife, Ethel Vincent, a dozen years later. The irrepressible Theresina, Viscountess Avonmore, traversed the continent in 1874, and in 1879 so did George Augustus Sala. All of them left long and varied accounts of their experiences, which help to form a picture of the newly united States in one of its most interesting decades.

We start, as they did, in New York – already one of the great cities of the world, with a million citizens as big as Berlin and destined shortly to become the distant magnet for millions more across the Atlantic. Sala, who had last seen New York during the Civil War, was amazed at its phenomenal growth[26]:

When I came here first (1863) Twenty-fifth street was accounted as being sufficiently far 'up-town' and Fortieth street was Ultima Thule. Beyond that the course of town lots planned out and prospected, but structurally yet to come, was only marked by boulders of the living rock having weird graffiti eulogistic of the virtues of Drake's Plantation Bitters and Old Dr Jacob Townsend's Sarsaparilla. What has become of those strange stencillings on the living rock? Where I remembered wildernesses I now behold terraces after terraces of lordly mansions of brown stone, some with marble facades, others wholly of pure white marble. . . . Unless my friends in New York are laughing at me, this state of things architectural goes on up to One Hundred and Ninetieth street.

New York, with its wondrous Brooklyn Bridge and its millionaires' row on Fifth Avenue, was by now indeed a worthy testament to the success and validity of the East Coast's new business ethic – a form of social Darwinism, which proclaimed that, as in the jungle, the fittest survived. As its prophet, Herbert Spencer, advised, 'There cannot be more good done than that of letting social progress go on unhindered; and immensity of mischief in the artificial preservation of those least able to care for themselves.' Such was the creed which infused America's eye-dazzling industrial 'boom' (to use the latest catchword), which formed the bedrock for the imminent or achieved fortunes of the Vanderbilts, Morgans, Carnegies and Rockefellers. The ultimate refinement, of course, of Spencer's philosophy was monopoly, but

New York landmark under construction: the skeleton of Brooklyn Bridge in the mid-1870s. Begun in 1872, and illuminated with electricity after its completion in 1883, it became one of the earliest ingredients in modern New York's world-famous skyline.

YN TOBACCO INSPECTION

The problems of urban
transit solved? Above: Charles
T. Harvey demonstrates the amenity of his
new West Side and Yonkers Patent Railway
in 1867. Below: the Third Avenue Elevated
Railway, somewhat more sophisticated and
running the whole length of the city.
Below it ran the tram-cars which curiously
– remarks Mrs Vincent – only began to pay
their way after the arrival
of the 'Elevated'.

that was a problem for other decades (although the first Trust was formed in 1882, Standard Oil).

'In Boston they ask you what you know, in Philadelphia who you are,' observed Mrs. Vincent[38]. 'In New York they ask you what you have.' But underlying this materialistic concern (as Sala felt) was a justifiable pride in a society which permitted *anyone* unlimited dreams:

A juvenile American, earning a salary of, say, six dollars a week, whose ideas run in the proper channels and whose head is screwed on the right way, rarely looks at himself in the glass, after he has been fixed by the barber, without seeing reflected in the mirror the features of a future President of the United States . . . our young English business men are not ambitious about anything save in attaining excellence as cricketers, bicyclists and lawn-tennis players; whereas the young American appears to be continually possessed by a settled purpose and determination to do something and become something 'big'.

It was a wholesome, and practical enough, vision, even if the 'big' men in New York were not always immaculate examples. In 1871, the city was run from Tammany Hall by a Democratic administration under William Tweed, a bankrupt but five years before, who could now sport diamond shirt-studs, a spectacular mansion, yacht and carriage. For some time the *New York Times* had publicly been pressing Boss Tweed to instruct them 'in the art of growing rich in as many years as can be counted on the fingers of one hand', and hinting at 'monstrous abuses of city funds, corrupt bargains with railroad sharpers, outrageous plots to swindle the general community'. But for a long time the *Times* was just whistling in the dark, convinced of its righteousness but hamstrung by lack of evidence (Tweed had even produced a committee of respectable businessmen to endorse a set of 'accounts' a few days before the city elections – which swept him and his omnivorous crew back into power). Then, that summer, came a break for the newspaper. A complete set of the real city accounts was handed in by one of Tweed's disaffected stooges, and they made fairy-story reading: the treasury had obviously been pillaged on a scale unknown since the sack of Rome. The *Times* printed the stupendous revelations in punctilious detail, including the news of a court-house 'plastered' at a cost of nearly $3 million, and offices 'altered' by a carpenter at something like $27,000 a day! That was the end of the Tweed Ring – the mayor, the controller, the Boss himself and their 'despicable and unclean herd' – but no one ever precisely discovered of how much New Yorkers had been cheated: there were those who put the figure as high as $200 million.

Frauds such as this – and the very next year the murder of speculator Jim Fisk directed public attention to yet another scandal in the manipulation of Erie Railroad stock – were about as relevant, however to the bulk of the city's population as the great Delmonico's (with its world-famous Baked Alaska) to the fifteen-cent houses with their standard fare of meat, fries and pickles. For the steady tide of immigrants was becoming, in the 1870s, a deluge: each year they arrived in their hundreds of thousands. Many of them moved on, the Germans to open up a shop in Cincinnati, or the Irish to labour in Boston; but many stayed, buoyant with hope but destitute or homeless. Conditions in many of the tenement blocks were appalling, as Sala found near the Bowery: 'The yard is in an abominable condition and the rooms, the upper of which are reached by external staircases, are but little better. Every inch of the walls and ceilings is as black as ink. . . . In some of the rooms the horrible odour of rottenness is sufficient to knock one down; and only those habituated to such pestilent smells could exist in the place.'

That particular quarter was Italian, but the consuming problem

Right: America's most distinguished and prolific inventor: Thomas Alma Edison at work in his laboratory. Modern technology owes an enormous debt to his work in the 1870s: in 1872 he perfected the duplex telegraph, and in 1876 the phonograph. In 1880 he constructed the first practical electric light – two years later his generating station in Pearl Street, New York, was in operation.

Left: Phineas T. Barnum, who with his partner Bailey opened their circus in Brooklyn in 1871 and styled it 'the greatest show on earth'. On his left two of their star attractions: the midgets Colonel and Mrs Tom Thumb. On the other side: Commander Nutt.

lay in the Irish – half a million arrived in the 1870s to swell the million and a quarter who had already fled the famines and terrorism of their homeland in the previous twenty years. But they did not shed their nationalism easily, importing their Orange and Shamrock feuds to the East River or collecting in secret Fenian covens. Virtually all were unskilled and ill-adapted to big-city life, and found themselves supplying the bulk of the domestic servants – a calling they scarcely relished, it seems. 'Servants are particularly wanting in due deference and respect,' remarked Viscountess Avonmore petulantly[1], '. . . and these, male and female, are all Irish servants. No people in the world are at home more obsequious to their masters than the poor Irish dependants and servants, and no class of people more arrogant and self-asserting when they become Americanized.'

From New York a number of excursions offered themselves to our intrepid tourists, before they plunged overland. There was Boston, which appealed to the Viscountess for its cultural heritage and the long literary shadows cast by its aging lions, Ralph Waldo Emerson and Henry Longfellow.

Mrs Vincent, though, chose to see Niagara Falls, impelled by Anthony Trollope's endorsement of them as carrying off the palm among all the natural wonders of the world. She was duly moved by the spectacle, but her visit was clouded by the news that, shortly before, the redoubtable Captain Webb (the same who had become the first man to swim the Channel in 1875) had been drowned while attempting to swim the rapids. There was some consolation, however, in that 'the enterprising owners of the restaurant at the rapids have arranged with his widow to come over during the season to sell photographs opposite the spot where her husband perished.'

The first stage of the daunting trip to the West was to Chicago, and there on, for the ordinary traveller, the unrelieved prospect of wooden seats and panic-stricken pauses at desolate halts for refreshment. But in the 1870s the better-heeled could temper the hardships a little by booking into one of Mr Pullman's Hotel Cars, whose carpets, leather-bound chairs and mahogany fascias moved even the hardbitten *New York Times* to fulsomeness: 'Upon tables covered with snowy linen and garnished with services of solid silver, Ethiop waiters, flitting about in spotless white, placed as if by magic a repast at which Delmonico himself could have had no occasion to blush.' Then, replete with antelope steak, mountain-brook trout and bumpers of Krug, the company, apparently, withdrew to the drawing-room car for a spot of choral singing: '. . . the voices of the men singers and of the women singers blending sweetly in the evening air, while our train, with its great glaring Polyphemus eye lighting up long vistas of prairie, rushed out into the night and the West.' The Viscountess Avonmore, doubtless with more of an eye for such things, espied no

The Statue of Liberty in unaccustomed stance, mid-1880s. Prompted as a gift from republican France to her exemplars in America in 1876, the statue took 10 years' work by the sculptor Bartholdi, and was shipped piecemeal across the Atlantic. It was unveiled, before hundreds of thousands, by President Cleveland in November, 1886.

silver whatsoever – 'the fittings, lamps, bolts, hinges, door-handles etc. were of the white metal called pinchbeck,' she pointed out, adding her strictures about the democratic form of sleeping accommodation, a form of communal dormitory with only flimsy curtains to salvage a lady's modesty. 'You have to go to bed in your boots – at least ladies have, and indeed they cannot undress at all because they cannot shroud themselves behind the curtains without placing themselves in a recumbent position . . .'

Still, a civilized night's sleep was guaranteed in Chicago, at the Grand Pacific, the Palmer House, the Sherman or any of the vast and palatial establishments that adorned the Windy City, and where even the hotel clerks seemed to Sala to wear diamonds 'as big as potatoes'. Everything was big in Chicago, her lumber mills, her stockyards, her grain elevators, Mr Armour's meat-packing factories – all testifying to the Mid-West's gathering momentum. And the more remarkable for the fact that in 1871 the greater part of the city had been destroyed by fire (the 'biggest' in America, of course). The fire, which started on the evening of 8 October, was fanned by an unusually strong wind and accelerated by weeks of drought. Having devoured miles of wooden suburban houses and timberyards, it turned hungrily on the great stone buildings of the commercial centre, where it consumed irresistibly through the night and all through the next day. All the great landmarks dissolved: the *Tribune* office, Crosby's Opera House (one of the nation's finest), the newly-renovated McVicker's Theatre, the magnificent Central Depot, hotels, churches, banks, and over three square miles of homes. There was $200 million-worth of damage, and half the fire offices in the Union went bankrupt overnight.

But with indomitable will the rebuilding started the moment the ruins were cool, and not even another serious fire in July 1874 could quench its renaissance – nor could even the legion of lurid laments and heroic couplets which the tragedy inspired in every paper in the land.

From the reborn Queen of the West the railroad stretched on to Omaha, which was the western terminus of the Union Pacific, on through the boundless prairies, to Cheyenne and Laramie. Once these plains had been black with the buffalo herds, roaming wild and free. To the Comanches, Sioux, Cheyenne, Pawnee these herds had been their life-blood, their food, clothing and shelter: to the settlers and railway-builders they were a stampeding nuisance, which could only be cured by a process of systematic extinction. True, trespassing on the great buffalo runs had its dangers, and the beasts had been known to attack a waggon-train like a cavalry charge, splintering it to pieces. 'They also object,' the Viscountess was told, 'to their projects being interfered with by the railroad, and sometimes when the train crosses their path they attack it *en masse*.' But the railroad had proved a more formidable foe, first by splitting the herds into two, north and

" SHIP YARD, JEFFERSONVILLE, IND.

Above: A steamer packed with cotton bales arrives at Jeffersonville quay.
Left: Silver Springs, Florida in the mid-1880s. Even in the new era of
transcontinental railroads, the rivers remained an important means of
communication – and a source of entertainment. The 'Showboat' business
flourished in the post-war years, some of the boats seating more than 2,000 in
style (even if the clientèle was often liable to arrive on board 'with a pistol in one
pocket, a whiskey flask in the other and a bowie knife in the boot'). In particular
the river trade began to revive with the slowly recovering cotton plantations.

Overleaf: Canal Street in 1870, crowded heart of cosmopolitan New Orleans,
a perpetual traffic-jam (as Sala notes) of horse-drawn trams. They interfered
ruthlessly, he complained, 'with the private comfort of people who do not want
to ride in tramway cars. In New Orleans you *must*. There is no way out of it.
Gentlemen go out to dinner, ladies go to balls per horse-car. It is the great
leveller – and be hanged to it, and its wheels, and its bells, and its plodding mule
to boot! . . . The horse-cars are down on you at any instant, almost of your
existence. An extended system of switches enables the vehicles to pirouette with
a nimbleness which is positively distracting, and which perpetually exposes the
foot passenger to the contingency of being run over.'

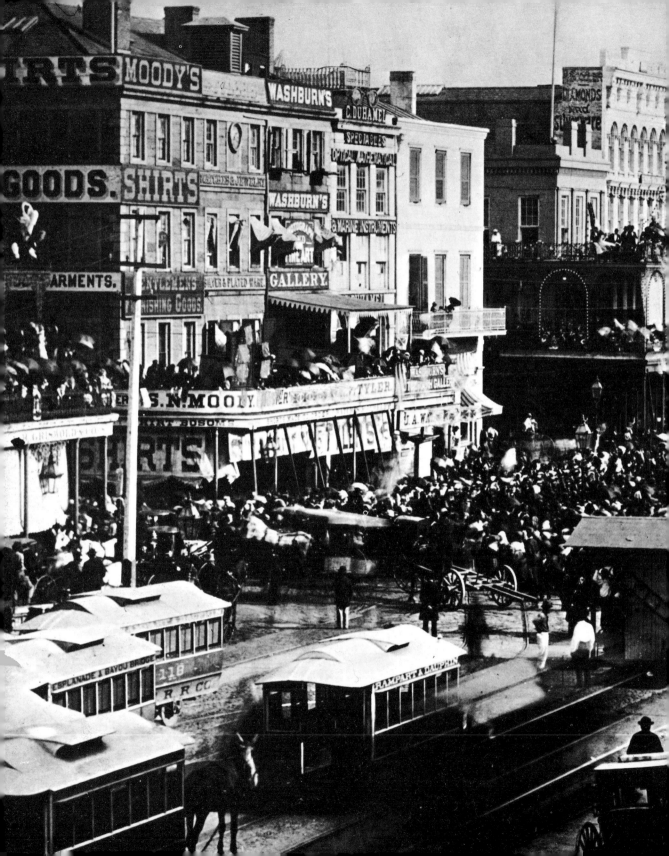

south, then by transporting the hunters to their very doorstep.

By the 1870s buffalo-hunting had turned from a sport into a massacre. 'Large shooting parties frequently do not even leave the cars. For the buffaloes literally cover the plain, and can be shot from the platform and windows – a sort of cockney sport, but one which the American hunter seems to delight in. Sometimes the plains are blackened over with these animals, and shooting at them is like firing into a mountain . . .' Between 1872 and 1874 an estimated three million animals were butchered for the paltry value of their skins (about two dollars), and in a few more years the herds had utterly vanished from the face of the prairies. And with them went the last hopes of the Plains Indians.

Even in the wake of the Civil War, Indian resentments had obliged the government to keep 25,000 troops in the field, and had made life in the more remote pioneering regions an armed nightmare. The long process of attrition by the usurper against the redman was nearing its inglorious conclusion: he had been herded off his birthright, the great hunting-grounds of his fathers, and corralled into sterile reservations, where he was magically expected to acquire the arts of husbandry. That he would submit to these barren acres and decrees of Washington willingly was wishful thinking, as the long epilogue of

Right: John Wesley Powell, one-time school-teacher and soldier, became one of America's great scientific leaders and first director of the Bureau of American Ethnology. His geological surveys (between 1867 and 1879) of the plateaux and canyons of the Rocky Mountain regions were examples of painstaking research and considerable courage – regardless of having lost his right arm during the Civil War he became the first man to navigate the Grand Canyon.

Below: The elusive 'frontier': a mule train pulls in to a typical pioneering town on the edge of the Rocky Mountains. Main Street, Helena, Montana, in 1874.

A threshing gang in Walsh County, North Dakota: mechanization in the late seventies and early eighties began to transform the face of the Prairies. The new twine-binder (over 15,000 were sold in 1882), seed-drills and straddle row cultivators vastly increased the acreage of production. But for the homesteaders of Custer County (below) ploughshares and prayers remained their only weapons against the prolonged droughts.

violence in the 1870s demonstrated. More than two hundred actions were fought in those years – the most renowned being George Custer's 'last stand' at Little Big Horn against Crazy Horse and Sitting Bull in 1876. Peering from her carriage window, Viscountess Avonmore in 1874 might have considered it a picturesque addition to the landscape to see 'a number of Indians on the war-path, dressed in all the glory of feathers, skins and scarlet blankets, leading their horses in single file over a frozen stream . . .' But the breech-loaders and repeaters, heritages of the Civil War, had swung the odds heavily against the Indian's shortbow, so that five years later Sala could only find tattered vagrants begging handouts at railway stations to whom 'the white post-traders sell poisonous whiskey and cheat in every conceivable manner, while the white squatter crowds him out by stealing the land assigned for Indian occupancy by the United States. . . . Those who do not sympathize with the Indian content themselves with asserting that he has got "to move out of the way or take the consequences".'

It wasn't only the buffaloes and Indians, though, who were brusquely invited to 'move out of the way'. The transcontinental railroads (by 1884 the Santa Fé, the North and South Pacifics had all completed overland routes) were rapidly turning the brutal realities of the wild west, with its impromptu justice and vigilantes, into romantic history: by the end of the seventies Kansas, Nebraska and

The last of the herds: hunters skin a buffalo in Montana, 1882. In years gone by these plains had been the home of millions of buffalo: now only a few had survived man's onslaught.

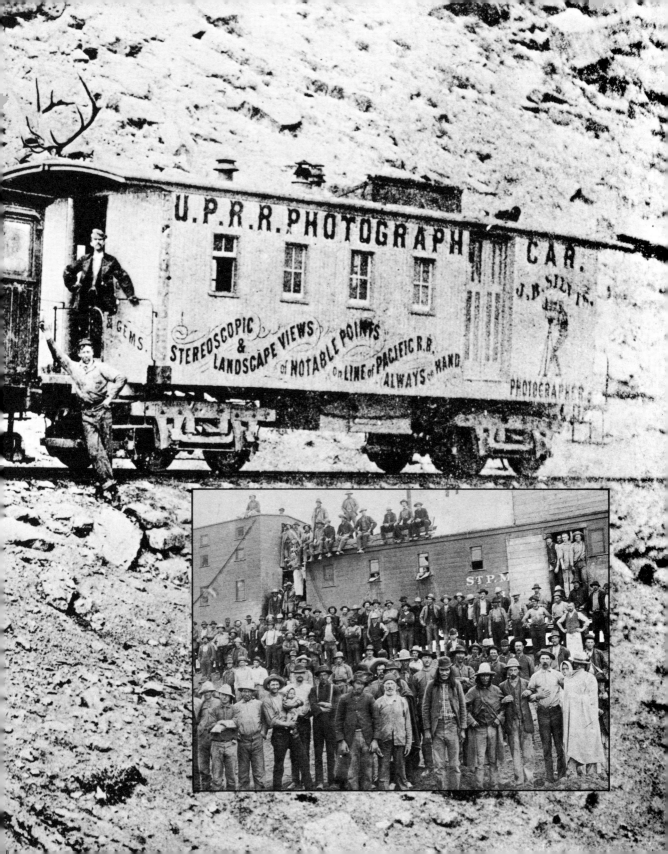

Colorado were all incorporated States, and within another ten years Wyoming, Washington, the Dakotas, and Idaho had all made the transition from 'territories'. Not only had the railroads put the stage-coaches, waggon trains and legendary Pony Express riders summarily out of business, they were at the same time initiating the now-familiar spiral of settlement and commercial development all along the way. A line running through inhabited country was better business than one in a wilderness, and immigrants thronged to buy up the bargain parcels of land which the generously-endowed rail companies now offered. (Posters and pamphlets advertising the unsurpassed attractions of life on the range found their way all over Europe in the 1870s, from the highlands of Scotland to the forest-villages of Bavaria; copywriters vied with each other in extolling Colorado, 'The Switzerland of America . . . a sure panacea for nearly every human ill', as against Minnesota where 'rich treasures were hid in the bosom of the New Earth' and a man could 'exchange the tyrannies and thankless toil of the old world for freedom and independence'.)

But (as in Australia) the new homesteaders found they had to contend not only with the vagaries of the elements – many saw they had been misled by the exceptional rainfall of the late sixties and gave up; others persevered in the common belief that 'rain would follow the plough' – but also with the proprietary instincts of the cattle barons, who objected to the enclosure of God's pasturelands and might register their objections with hired guns. It was a long-standing confrontation which owed its outcome, in the settlers' favour, as much to the invention of barbed wire (in 1874) as to the gradual encroachment of law and order.

Whatever other social unorthodoxies may have been practised at the next important settlement along the railroad, Salt Lake City, lawlessness was *not* one of them. This curious community had grown into a city of over 100,000 in the thirty years since Joseph Smith, Brigham Young and their dedicated band of Mormons, persecuted out of the East, had lighted on their Promised Land beyond the Wasatch Mountains. Whether intense proselytizing or polygamy accounted for this rich harvest was a matter of great speculation on both sides of the Atlantic – and now that the railroad stopped nearby, Salt Lake City had become an irresistible tourist-stop, either for the abandoning or reinforcement of one's prejudices. Sala came, saw and remained unconquered.

I do not think that I am wandering very far from the truth in making the general statement that the rank and file of the Mormons are a most laborious, peaceable, law-abiding and deservedly thriving community, and that they are kept in a state of spiritual subjection by a select ring of nasty old men who, by aid of a cunningly-devised theocracy and a preposterous theological humbug, are enabled to fill their purses and to gratify their libidinous propensities.

Possibly the difficulty of coming by a decent drink soured his

Previous pages: The 1870s and '80s saw the foundations of America's huge network of railroads laid – sometimes with astonishing speed. Right: This gang pushing a line westwards through Dakota and Montana (mid-1880s) laid almost 650 miles of track in one season. They lived in communal dormitory-cars, whose upper stories had to be sawn down, when mountain country was reached, to fit into tunnels. And everywhere the railroad went, the photographic car wasn't far behind. Above: the Union Pacific official photographer in Wyoming, 1869. Left: For passengers, the discomforts of several days' confinement could be tempered a little in one of Mr Pullman's palatial cars (c. 1870).

judgement, and he did admit himself baffled at the extent of true polygamy: 'I was told that it was always feasible to estimate the numerical strength of the seraglio of a Mormon Elder by the number of front doors of his house. The largest number of doors which I counted on the facade of a single dwelling was thirteen; but it would be, of course, imprudent to accept this as a sure test. In some cases there may not be a wife for every front door: in others there may not be a front door for every wife.' On the other hand, William Henry Seward arrived with an open mind, talked with Brigham Young (who admitted to nineteen wives, and an infinite number of spiritual ones 'sealed' to him for eternity) and left as uncommitted as he came[29]. 'If there was any jealousy among the wives,' he remarked, 'it's escaped our penetration.' But, he was bound to add, he didn't think polygamy very American and as soon as the Mormons abolished it they should command all men's toleration. He saw 'no reason to question Young's sincerity in his eccentric religious faith and practices', and deemed it unjust 'to deny him extraordinary ability, energy and perseverance as a founder of an American state'. That was the point. The United States in the Seventies, more than ever as minorities from the old world came to seek sanctuary, could not retreat from its proud tradition of toleration, whether a man be a Plymouth Brother, a Christian Scientist, a Swedenborgian, a Shaker, a Jehovah's Witness, or a Second Adventist.

From Salt Lake the train trundled on, weaving along the valley of the Humboldt till it reached the last great obstacle, the Sierra Nevada. There, to the Viscountess's horror, it 'creaked slowly over precarious-looking bridges, with hundreds of feet of yawning gulf beneath, and traversed ledges so fearfully narrow that if one had dropped a glove from the carriage window, it would have fallen straight three thousand feet!' Then (with her ladyship's wardrobe complete, one hopes) it descended into the Californian plain – and San Francisco. Before the '49 gold rush this had been a Spanish shanty village of a few hundred souls: now it was a great commercial centre of over three hundred thousand, solidly based on the prosperity of those who had struck it rich in the tributaries of the San Joaquin and Sacramento. Gone were the shanties and gambling halls, and in their place had risen an imposing, if ill-assorted, mixture of high civic architecture and bay-windowed suburbs, libraries, cathedrals, and Mr Sharon's world-famous Palace Hotel, offering a choice of 'European or American accommodation' and conducted tours into the Yosemite Valley.

The days of the diggings were over now, and mining had become a rich man's business with quartz-crushing machines and stamp-mills. But grizzled prospectors still swapped stories in the bars and get-

Below: The railroads
might be superseding the
gallant pony expresses,
but in outlying areas the
local stage still had its day:
Sand Springs, Nevada in
1867. Left: For the settlers
and their families home
might be a collection of
tents in the Californian
sunshine, or a house built
of sods in Custer County
(below left) – except this
family did not want to send
a photograph of their
spartan home to friends
back east, preferring to
prove they actually owned
an organ instead (1880s).

rich-quick schemes could be guaranteed an eager hearing. In 1872 the rumours were as strong as ever, and those with their ears to the ground told of a great diamond field, discovered by two strangers who had deposited a huge cache of them at a 'Frisco bank – and disappeared. In due course, they were found, their claim authenticated by one of the best-known mining men in California. An ambitious and eminently respectable company was floated, the New York and San Francisco Mining and Commercial Company. Diamond frenzy mounted to fever pitch.

It was, alas, a gigantic hoax, ingenious and carefully planned to make a killing on the San Francisco stock exchange. And it would have worked, but for the curiosity of Clarence King, then surveying the fortieth parallel (for these were the years of the great western surveys, of Hayden in Yellowstone, Powell among the canyons and plateaus). Piecing together fragmentary clues, King worked out the location of the 'diamond fields' which had been kept a close secret. He found diamonds, but on closer inspection it became clear that to have got there they would have had to defy the laws of nature; or, as one unhappy investor told the New York Times, it would have been easier 'for a person in San Francisco to toss a marble in the air and have it fall on Bunker Hill Monument'.

Along with earthquakes, ephemeral crises like this California could absorb: there were plenty of steadier routes to riches, such as growing the vines or oranges which flourished in the balmy Californian climate (advertised, Sala says, as 'eminently favourable to the cure of gunshot wounds'). But there was one perennial crisis that San Franciscans could not shrug off: the Chinese problem. As the Californian put it in 1879, 'There is a small but rapidly increasing province of the Chinese empire established on the Pacific coast . . . with its hideous gods, its horrible opium dens, its slimy dungeons and its concentrated nastiness of every kind.' Sala investigated the half square mile that comprised Chinatown on his own account, and could not find any excessive keenness of smell nor any need for the phial of aromatic vinegar he had been advised to take along. Indeed he found them 'indefatigably patient, laborious and neat-handed; willing to undertake the most toilsome and repulsive manual labour and the nicest arts and crafts.' Which was precisely what the working folk of the West objected to – the fact that Chinamen could, and would, work for fifty cents a day and still save something from the pittance. Labour demonstrations and outrages on the Chinese community grew commonplace, while anti-immigration groups flourished. One of them solicited the support of Mr Seward on his arrival in town, but he refused on the grounds that 'immigration and expansion are the main and inseparable elements of civilization of the American continent, and nowhere more needful or beneficent than on the Pacific coast.' Despite Mr Seward's admirable sentiments, they had their way. In

Photographic surveys in the Sierras in the 1870s called for patience and a head for heights.

117

Learning the hard way: the Velocipede Training College at Miles Bridge. The first American bicycles were manufactured by A. A. Pope in 1878, and became instantly popular. Seven years later a San Francisco man actually completed a round-the-world trip on one of these bone-grinding machines.

1882 Chinese immigration was banned for ten years.

As the cartoonists never tired of pointing out, there was a peculiar conflict in America's racial policies. On the West coast, the yellow man was hated because he didn't turn himself into a full-blooded American citizen: in the South, the black man was hated because he did. The abolition of slavery, in spite of the radical republicans' efforts, had not proved an undiluted blessing for the negro. True, many of them were now gaining the rudiments of an education and some notable negro colleges were being founded. True, the ex-slaves could now vote and sit in state legislatures. But, materially, they might have been forgiven for wondering exactly where the fruits of freedom lay, particularly those who still mouldered in government camps, or those who had turned to share-cropping and had mortgaged even the hopes of a cotton-harvest to their white southern landlord or their white northern supplier. The promised benefits of emancipation had proved illusory, for local 'black codes' had contrived to circumvent the best intentions of Washington and local white vigilantes made sure the codes were adhered to.

No one, white or black, except the rare war-profiteer, could claim to be prospering from reconstruction: there was no capital to set the old plantations back on their feet, there was a public debt (in 1874) of $125 million, a scourge of northern carpetbaggers came south to pick the bones of the old confederacy (as well as, in some states, a Union army of occupation propping up republican legislatures), and a free-labour market which no one could afford. It was cheaper to hire black convict labour than to take on freedmen – and many owners did so, thus reducing the 'free' rates to the level of the convicts. A great many whites were as impoverished as the negroes and, viewing the blatant corruption of reconstruction politics, looked wistfully back to the good old days of white supremacy.

Some even took it upon themselves to secure their imminent return, forming themselves into local guerrilla groups whose appellations, 'red shirts' or 'rifle club', but thinly disguised their objectives. The most militant of these was the Ku Klux Klan, with its nightriders, its white masks and fiery crosses, and mystical mumbo-jumbo. As life became increasingly perilous for the freedmen, a full-scale exodus began to the West, which Sala observed as he travelled back across the continent.

The garments of the new-comers were terribly tattered and patched, and there was in all likelihood not a dollar in money in the pockets of the entire party. They were speedily followed by new arrivals [this is in Kansas] and before a fortnight had elapsed their number had increased to upwards of a thousand, all of them pitifully poor and hungry, many of them sick . . . although they resolutely declared with convincing emphasis that nothing would induce them to return to the South . . . there being no security for their lives and property in their old homes, the laws and courts being alike inimical to them, and the exercise of the electoral franchise being obstructed and made a personal danger to them.

It seemed as if the whole of America, as Sala observed, was 'in a state of flux, of restlessness'. At times it might be the restlessness of discontent – economically the slump that followed a disastrous financial panic in 1873 brought hardship to most levels of society almost till the end of the decade – but viewed from the Old World it was infinitely preferable to the passive discontent at home that sapped the will of the oppressed. When Sala re-embarked at New York in 1880 for his homeward journey, the dockside was crowded with the first of another five million immigrants the new decade was to bring.

Even after the American Civil War the rapidly re-uniting States had not entirely abandoned the dream of an all-embracing America, stretching from Mexico to the North West territories. The Americans, as one of their politicians put it, 'had a great swaller for territory' and this, after all, seemed to them a logical expansion. With the purchase of Alaska from Russia in 1867, only British Columbia stood in the way of complete American control of the West Coast, and the long continental frontier – what with vindictive Fenians continually crossing it to create havoc and outrage in the north – was at best an embarrassment. What was more, the Americans felt, annexation would have been no less than the British deserved for allowing Confederate privateers to operate from Canadian ports. Already the treaty for reciprocal trade across the frontier, which had stood since 1854, had been denounced by the United States as a mark of their disapproval.

But the mood of Canadians – even those who feared they might be ultimately left in the lurch by Britain – was decidedly not for falling like a ripe plum into the American basket, but rather for self-determination. In 1867, the great sprawling territories of British North America took the first step towards federation, when four provinces (Quebec, Ontario, New Brunswick and Nova Scotia) were established as the Dominion of Canada. That left a lot of territory outside the pale, of course – much of it implacably opposed to federation, like Newfoundland, which had to wait another eighty years, and like the Red River settlement in the backwoods, where Louis Riel and the Metis tried to set up their own independent government.

Riel's rebellion collapsed in 1870, and the new province of Manitoba was duly carved out of the muddy forests and prairies. Between there and the Rockies stretched vast untrodden 'districts' (now the provinces of Alberta and Saskatchewan) and, beyond, the old, sophisticated and very British colony of Columbia. Not until 1871 were the Columbians persuaded to join the Dominion, and only then on the understanding that a trans-Canada railroad would be a first

Below: Sightseers come to view the wondrous ice-mountain formed by a frozen Niagara Falls.

Above: A monumental man-made ice palace erected in Dominion Square, Montreal in 1884.

Overleaf: A lumber camp in the Ottawa District, 1871.

priority. Two years later little Prince Edward Island also joined, bowing to the inevitable as it watched the debts incurred by its railroad contracts mounting out of sight.

Though not completed until 1885, the Canadian Pacific Railway was in fact the vital artery that pumped life into the new federation: it was, as one historian commented, like a skewer holding together all the disparate provinces like so many pieces of kebab. The project was for ever tottering on the brink of bankruptcy, and so slow was progress that British Columbia at one stage threatened to secede. But it was also a tremendous human achievement in extremes of temperature and over some of the most dangerous terrain in the world. Mary FitzGibbon, an engineer's wife, spent two years in the remote fastnesses observing the primitive and dangerous life of the railroadworkers, and left a vivid description of the daily hazards[12], bears and rapids, forest fires and dynamite, swamps and ice-drifts. The prohibition laws were doubtless an additional burden, but fairly safe to flaunt (Mrs FitzGibbon reports), since in winter the nearest jail to the railroad was more than a hundred impassable miles away.

The work and pay attracted 'navvies of every nation; tall, brawny Scotchmen; jolly-looking Irishmen, stumpy little French Canadians, solemn, stupid-looking Icelanders . . .' These last she studied with interest, concluding that they were

lethargic-looking, with bright milk-and-roses complexions, great opaque blue eyes, and a heavy gait that gives them an appearance of stupidity which is not a true index

of their character. . . . They are teachable servants, neat, clean and careful, but have not constitutional strength to endure hard work. The grass-hopper plague which visited Manitoba during two consecutive seasons destroyed their crops, and the ravages of smallpox during the fall of '76 and spring of '77 told upon them so severely that they have so far only been an expense to the Canadian Government.

Some of the Indians too, she notes, had come to rely on the white man's gratuities, whether it be the shelter of some desolate mission or else treaty-money from the Hudson Bay trading-posts. But they seemed happy, their birch-bark wigwams clean if sparse, and their velvet-dressed, braided children contrasting slightly oddly with their painted medicine-men and their tom-toms. The other community that inspired her curiosity were the Mennonites, sedate and gravely polite. 'They are all,' she claimed, 'thrifty and energetic, and make excellent settlers', a sentiment which the Governor-General's wife, Lady Dufferin, echoed and expanded on[10]

One hundred and twenty families arrived in Canada three years ago [the first had arrived nearly a hundred years earlier in fact] and settled on this bare prairie one autumn day . . . having left Russia for conscientious reasons, in the same way that they left their native land, Germany, because they will not fight and these two countries require that their subjects should serve in the army. They are most desirable emigrants; they retain their best German characteristics, are hard-working, honest, sober, simple, hardy people; they bring money into the country . . . and everybody has at least six children.

That was indeed an admirable colonial virtue, for the Canadian plains offered no short cuts to affluence: they called for hard toil and the work of many hands. Many came in the Seventies and Eighties and were discouraged by soil they did not know how to farm, by diseases and short seasons they could not cope with, and by the depression which undermines agricultural prices across the world. Emigration in these two decades (largely to the United States) far outstripped immigration, and only natural increase kept development going after the homestead 'boom', which the new railroad brought to Winnipeg, Regina and Calgary, collapsed. Yet for the more dedicated – as Mrs FitzGibbon discovered perseverance could bring its rewards:

Many of the vegetables were so large that a description of them was treated with incredulity until some specimens were sent to Ottawa, to be modelled for the Philadelphia Centennial Exhibition. One Swedish turnip weighed over thirty-six pounds; some potatoes measured nine inches long and seven in circumference; radishes were a foot and a half long and four inches round; kail branched out to the size of a currant bush.

But if westward progress was gentle it was also orderly, particularly after the formation of the redoubtable North West Mounted Police in 1874; and elsewhere industries sprang up, such as the new salmon-canning business, which augured well for the Dominion's future. Lady Dufferin, as intrepid a tobogganer and as ardent an amateur

Life in the wilderness. Above: Lumbermen loading logs from a skidway on to a sleigh, 1871. Below: Local Indians at New Westminster, British Columbia (1870s), adapting to the white man's ways.

thespian as you could hope to find, found the society of larger towns congenial. Her chatty diaries follow her viceregal progresses across the continent: to Quebec and Montreal where grand municipal buildings were already jostling with the quaint gabled French houses and crooked streets; to Toronto, the most English of towns, where the affairs of the British Parliament were pored over at the breakfast table, news of debates always arriving in time for the first edition, and where 'the comfortable wooden houses of the upper and middle orders convey an idea of prosperity, with their neat gardens, a swinging hammock in the creeper-covered verandah and the family sitting out in the cool of the evening'; and to Ottowa, whose great pile of minaret-gothic Parliament buildings towered along the waterfront – and in which, Lady Dufferin maintained, you were as likely to hear snatches of 'La Marseillaise' as of 'God Save the Queen'.

Wherever the Dufferins travelled (during their tour of duty 1872–6) a social maelstrom immediately seemed to brew up – impromptu curling matches, skating parties, hunts, tableaux vivants, fancy-dress balls. In the face of their enthusiasm French and English rivalries seemed to dissolve and Catholic-Protestant disputes abate. Her hopeful journals may have been, in reality, a gloss on the uncompromising struggles of those early years, but as an epitaph to their tour she quotes a speech of her husband which – she says – earned five minutes of standing ovation from his distinguished audience.

Never has the head of any Government passed through a land so replete with contentment, so pregnant of promise in the future. From the northern forest border lands to the wheat-laden townships that smile along the Lakes; from the orchards of Niagara to the hunting-grounds of Nipigon . . . everywhere I have learnt that the people are satisfied with their own individual prospects and with the prospects of their country; satisfied to be subjects of the Queen; satisfied to be members of the British Empire.

Australia : Self-Discovery

The Cobb & Co. stage-coach, near Gulgong, N.S.W. in 1871.

The trouble with Australians, Anthony Trollope complained, was that they were great 'blowers', for ever trumpeting the praises of their beautiful cities, their grand public monuments, their agricultural wealth and incomparable mineral resources. And indeed it was only natural, from the far side of the world, for imperialists like Trollope to adopt such a slightly cynical, avuncular attitude towards those precocious colonies which not so very long before had been convict depôts. Even the indulgent *Times*, commenting on the sizeable loans dispensed to the colonies, referred to them as 'English charity', in a tone of voice that clearly implied London was unlikely to see much of it back.

The view from Australia, needless to say, was very different – even to a well-bred Frenchman, Edmond La Meslée, who landed in the Antipodes in 1876. 'Ah, dear Mr Trollope! Let them have their say,' he insisted[20]. 'They are not so far wrong after all; for no country in the world, not even America in proportion to its population, can show such astonishing progress. . . . And then they are a young people with the faults of youth. Let them shout, therefore, "We have done this! We have done that!" What harm is there in it? . . . All in all,' he concluded, 'the Australians are good fellows. They have excellent qualities; and who is without faults?' At any rate La Meslée was content to settle in the new country, and eventually became one of the founders of the Australian Geographical Society. And he was right – the Australians in the 1870s *did* have something to boast about.

Just twenty years had passed since South Australia and Victoria had been given representative government. Then Melbourne had been a village: now it was a busy, geometric city of 200,000 souls extending over a radius of nearly ten miles, with huge government buildings in the Italian style, a university, botanical gardens and a string of fashionable bathing-resorts on its doorstep. Even little Brisbane, a rough-and-ready convict depôt until Queensland had been granted separate colonial status a mere ten years earlier, now snaked importantly along the river and round its high-domed Parliament House. Even more to the point, three of the colonies had adopted universal suffrage long before democratic America, and Victorians were old hands at the secret ballot when Whitehall was still agonizing over its ethics.

So when it was announced in the autumn of 1867 that the Queen's second son, Prince Alfred, Duke of Edinburgh, was arriving on an Official Tour, the settlers might perhaps have been forgiven – even in their pleasure at the prospect – for furiously embarking on a debate in the press as to whether the real purpose of the Prince's visit was not to distribute honours to prominent citizens. It was not, as it turned out: but it was one of the very earliest of a series of royal odysseys designed to emphasize the integrity of Britain's sprawling empire (the first, to Canada, had been undertaken by the

Prince of Wales a few years before). And in that respect the tour was signally successful, to judge by the hundredweights of illuminated, vellum-backed Declarations of Loyalty taken aboard HMS *Galatea*. The Prince's chaplain, the Reverend Milner who kept a meticulous journal of the tour[21], lost count of the number of be-mottoed triumphal arches the entourage was obliged to drive through, and of monumental gas-lit transparencies of His Highness (so hastily and hazily constructed that even the easy-going Prince murmured to his chaplain, 'I do not think Mother would recognise me').

Each rival colony strove to outdo the other – for the days of Federation were still a long way ahead – not only in the lavishness of its welcome, Milner noted sourly, but also in the length of its speeches. Some events were an unqualified success, like the spectacular naval welcome in Sydney harbour; some were bizarre, like the nervous effort to floodlight Melbourne's parliament building with a stubborn set of galvanic batteries, or like the *al fresco* lunch at Randwick races which included roast alpaca, grilled wonga pigeons, plovers' eggs and rock oyster pie; and some were disasters, such as the ill-fated Melbourne Free Banquet.

Early in the morning of this philanthropic gesture by the patricians of Melbourne towards the deserving poor, the seeds of impending catastrophe were visible when some 70,000 persons began assembling for a feed prepared for, at the most, a tenth of that number. Informed of the possible danger to life and limb in such a crush the Prince wisely decided to remain aboard the *Galatea* – but no one informed the organizers. After three or four hours of commendable patience in the dusty heat the mob went berserk and fell upon the laden tables 'like a great sea of pent-up waters'. It was, reported the *Melbourne Argus,* 'a bacchanalian picture such as we shudder to recall, a frightful saturnalia of unbelievable horror, set against a general background of struggling carnivora'.

Nevertheless everyone was beginning to congratulate themselves that the tour as a whole had been a credit to Australia when a real calamity occurred. On 12 March 1868 at a public picnic in Clontarf overlooking Sydney harbour, an assassination attempt was made on the Prince. An Irishman, James O'Farrell, fired into his back at close range and only failed to kill him because of the prompt reactions of the bystanders and the Prince's stout braces which deflected the bullet away from his spine. Although O'Farrell continued to deny it, even in his death-cell, it was universally assumed that this was yet another of those Fenian outrages which the English newspapers were full of, and a disturbing outbreak of anti-Irish hysteria followed.

The Prince mercifully survived to return home, and eventually to mount the throne of tiny Saxe-Coburg-Gotha, leaving behind him a welter of foundation-stones for schools, docks, town halls and hospitals which augured well for the colonies' progress, if not for

Free enterprise in the outback: Beaufoy Merlin's portrait of Charley Bird and his patent medicine emporium at Home Rule, New South Wales (1871), which also served as sorting-office for Matthew the Bellman, local town crier and postman.

Overleaf: J. Kennedy's unprepossessing haven for sartorially-minded miners at Hill End in the 1870s— a survivor of the booming days of the gold rush.

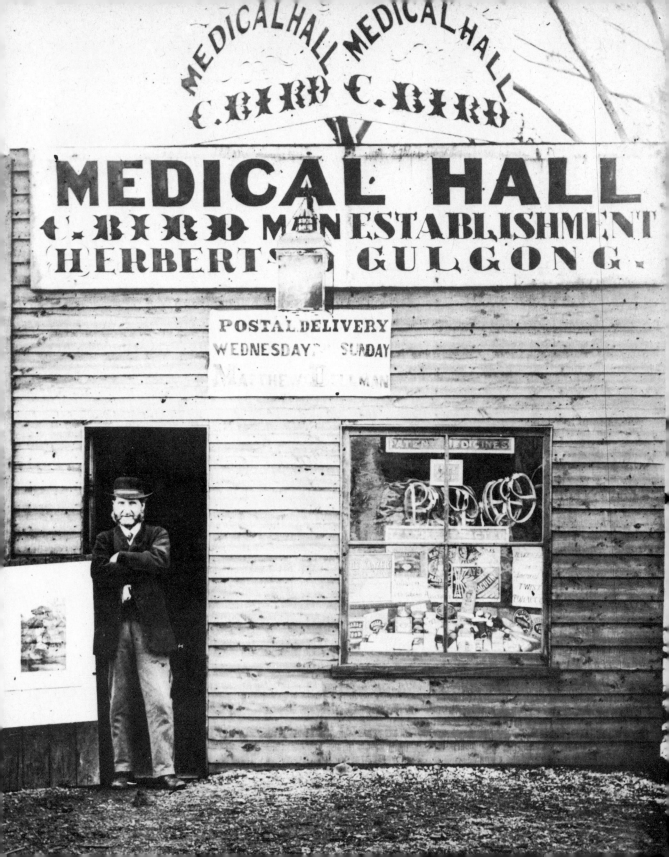

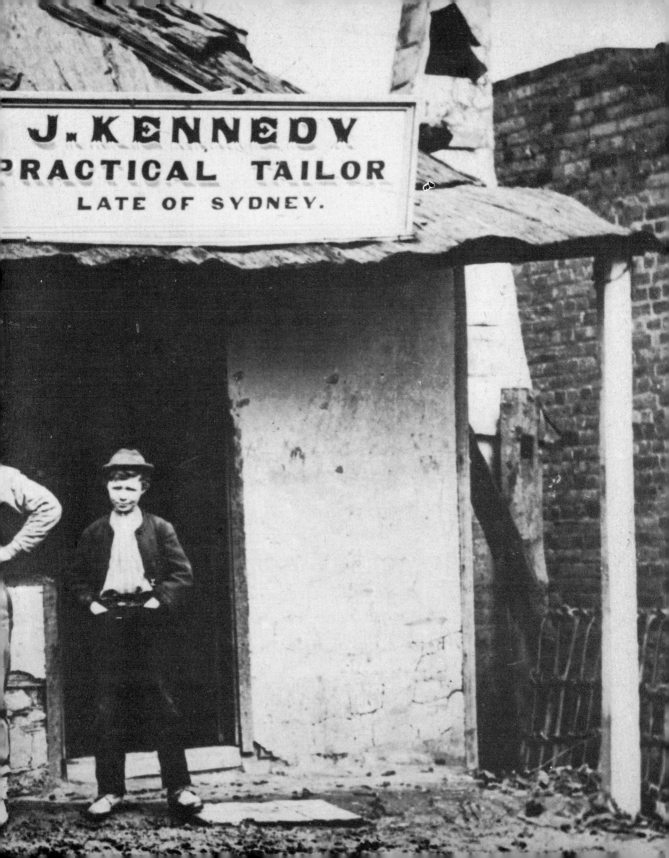

Memory of golden days: miners in camp in Western Australia, 1870s. By the end of the 60s the mining population had dwindled to half and the Golden Decade was over—remaining alluvial deposits of gold proved to be too far from water, and quartz reefs strictly for the professional. Many abandoned their claims for the newer and more promising rewards of the sheep stations and big farms.

their pockets. It might have seemed to Prince Alfred, whirled from ballroom to banqueting hall and race-course to regatta, that Australia was a land of perpetual fun. If it did, then it was only because the bunting and the banners which hung so limp on his departure had successfully curtained off the hard realities.

For Australia did not yield its secrets or its riches easily. The waves of gold fever that during the past two decades had washed over the country, throwing up towns like Ballarat and Castlemaine, had receded somewhat, leaving behind only companies with enough capital to dig deep into the quartz reefs and enough faith to go on searching for their two-ounces-a-ton, or else leathery prospectors grimly sieving the dust of the alluvial plains until they had amassed sufficient gold-dirt to send them on a 'spree'. La Meslée was constantly inveighing against this established Australian tradition which so often made his travels a misery: 'About midnight the Royal Mail coach arrived, full to overflowing. They were miners returning from a newly discovered field which had been abandoned for lack of water. They were all more or less drunk, and throughout the night they kept up the most infernal din I have ever heard in my life. Never, most emphatically never, have I heard such language as assailed my ears all that night. . . .'

Another eye-witness to these debauches, George Baden Powell, explained the routine to would-be emigrants from Britain[2]:

A sort of notion gets the better of him [the miner] that what he has earned is as nothing to what he can easily earn afterwards . . . therefore he retires to the nearest public, hands his money over to the landlord, bidding him tell him when all is finished. He will then live there, probably, continuously more or less drunk, and in that state forcing all who enter to drink at his expense. When all is spent the landlord informs the man, who leaves contentedly; and should he carry with him a bottle of grog, handed to him at the last moment by the host, he will sing said landlord's praises all over the country.

It was this kind of man, Baden Powell went on, that having made a fortune in the old days only to fritter it away in England at a rate of £30,000 a year, fixed in the minds of immigrants the idea that 'they could arrive in Australia to live in clover and with but little work and stand to tumble somehow or other into a goodly fortune.' But for a level-headed member of the well-educated classes (with a remittance of perhaps £20 a quarter) Baden Powell could conceive of no more healthy existence than that of a 'squatter' in the great outback.

The life of a squatter – who rented vast tracts of territory from the Government, called runs, for the grazing of sheep or cattle – had its hardships, not least 'the notorious diet of everlasting mutton: roasted, boiled or stewed, there is still nothing but mutton.' But it also had potentially huge rewards: runs of over 100,000 sheep built up by men who had begun by building their own station out of canvas and gum-tree bark were by no means uncommon (by the end of the decade there were well over 60 million sheep being raised in Australia). And the wool and meat trades were booming, especially after 1879 when the process of freezing meat for shipment to Britain was perfected.

The squatters' most common enemy was the 'free-selector' or, as he was less politely called, 'cockatoo-farmer' in the pretence that those gentlemen could raise nothing better than white cockatoos, which swarmed wild over their properties. The 1870s witnessed a running war between these two sections of the community, usually bitter, often violent. The cause of the friction – perversely enough in a continent where boundless land was the big attraction – was that a free-selector, for the payment of £1 an acre to the Government or 5s down and the rest in instalments, could purchase the leasehold on any land he fancied, and inevitably he fancied the best parts of the squatters' runs where the grass was lush and the water ran clear. However long the squatter had been in possession of this land, however much he may have improved it by the sweat of his own brow, there was nothing legal he could do to prevent 'the eyes of his runs being picked out'.

Simple legislations could have remedied this evil, but governments seemed in a state of paralytic indecision as to what form this should take. Armchair politicians were for ever coming up with helpful suggestions, but in the meantime the most practical solution was for the squatter to wait for these 'gulley-takers' to go bust (which they often did) and buy up their land at a give-away price, or else to put up a friend deliberately to go bust and only lose the deposit.

Another hazard for remote communities in the bush were the bush-rangers, not the itinerant swagmen with blanket rolls round their necks (though doubtless they could be a lot less 'jolly' than modern folklore credits them) but marauding bandits, of whom the Kelly Gang were but one group, if the most notorious. In 1876 La Meslée's train en route to Brisbane stopped, he noted, at a little hamlet of four or five houses called Glenrowan. Four years later this sorry collection of shacks entered Australian history as the place where Ned Kelly and his men met their end.

Beseiged at last in the tumbledown 'hotel' where they had turned up for a local dance, the Kelly boys for hours kept up a desperate gunfight against police (breathlessly followed by citizens all over the continent with access to a telegraph). At one stage in the drama Ned appears in the open for a shoot-out with the law, in an iron vizor and suit of armour which for a time defies the police bullets, until one shot shatters his unprotected knee. His comrades inside hold out a little longer, only to be burned alive when the shanty goes up in flames like a tinderbox.

Ned Kelly rapidly became a folk-hero, just as other ruffians were

Outlaw's end: the body of Joe Byrne, member of the Ned Kelly gang, after it had been recovered from the burning Glenrowan Hotel (where Kelly and his men made their final stand against police), 1880. Kelly himself died on the gallows.

Overleaf: Bogged down in Clarke Street, Hill End, 1872.

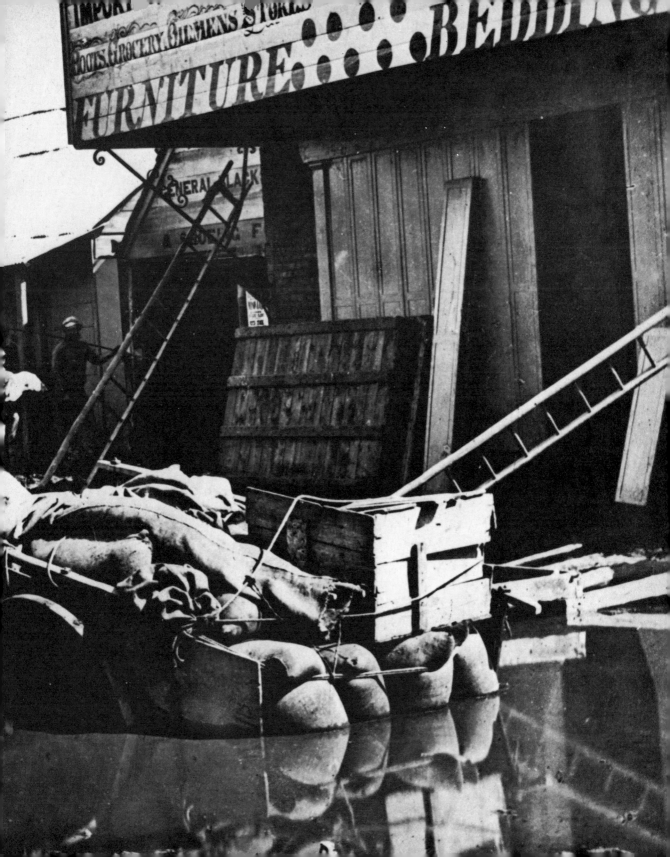

being beatified on America's frontier: petitions were raised to save him from the hangman, and betting was heavy that he would somehow cheat his fate (he didn't). To many of his contemporaries he seemed to epitomize, if in an extreme fashion, those gritty qualities a man needed to tame the bush – contempt for authority, fearlessness and self-reliance. These were qualities notably lacking, they claimed, in the aboriginals who also inhabited the frontiers (to call them 'natives' was considered to be an insult to immigrants of good English stock).

It was a summary judgment, and hardly fair, for the only aboriginals most Australians met were those debilitated by contact with the white man's civilization. In the 1870s there was a considerable (though rapidly dwindling) number of them still in their nobler and more savage state beyond the pale: although a telegraph line spanned the continent from north to south between Adelaide and Darwin, virtually the whole wilderness to the west of that was unknown territory. Few men had attempted to penetrate very far, and those who had not turned back in time had perished at the hands of (and very likely been eaten by) the aborigines. In 1874, the explorer John Forrest was the first to succeed in crossing the arid desert-plains from Perth to the telegraph line, and recorded in his journal[14] several near-fatal encounters with the cannibals.

Looking towards the hill I saw from forty to sixty natives running towards the camp, all plumed up and armed with spears and shields. I was cool, and told Sweeney to bring out the revolvers; descended from the tree and coo-eyed to Pierre and Kennedy, who came running. By this time they were within sixty yards, and halted. One advanced to meet me and stood twenty yards off; I made friendly signs; he did not appear very hostile. All at once one from behind (probably a chief) came rushing forward, and made many feints to throw spears. He went through many manoeuvres, and gave a signal, when the whole number made a rush towards us, yelling and shouting, with their spears shipped. . .

Such martial behaviour from an aboriginal would have come as a revelation to most Australians: in the townships it was a pathetically common sight to see them huddled round a grog-shop, begging sixpences to get drunk on and coughing their lungs out from the tobacco they accepted in payment for the little work they could do. They were all of them repulsively ugly and filthy, said La Meslée, having stumbled on an aboriginal encampment. 'Men and women, barely covered in veritable rags and tatters of decomposing woollen blankets, wandered about the camp. In the shelter of the huts, half enveloped in an ancient rag some old hag gnawed away at a kangeroo bone . . . never had I seen such a degrading spectacle, and I would never have believed that there were human beings capable of living in such a state of nastiness and misery.'

But having registered his horror or contempt, possibly even stopping to wonder how such a primitive species could have worked

out the sophisticated aerodynamics of the boomerang, the average immigrant would leave them to their own devices, acknowledging the empirical truth of Baden Powell's thesis: 'After one or two palpable evidences of the superior power of the white man, they are forced to recognize his supremacy. . . . If once the black commences loafing about the more civilized parts, he is sure to die off rapidly.'

More likely, his very special repugnance would be reserved for the 'almond-eyes'. Chinese immigration was an issue exercising authorities all over the world from Limehouse to San Francisco, but nowhere did it arouse more passion than in Australia. In spite of swingeing immigrant taxes laid upon them they continued to pour into the new country: this 'pig-tailed peril' (protested La Meslée, already displaying symptoms of a White Australia policy) 'like a Mongol horde hurling itself on the rich gold-bearing districts of North Queensland, thence to spread like a dangerous yellow plague over the whole surface of Australia'. They never brought their womenfolk, yet they multiplied as fast as rabbits (which had been first imported at about the same time); they were clannish and industrious, and worst of all they undersold the European. They

Above: The manager and staff of the Bank of New South Wales at Gulgong, 1870s.

Previous pages: The first pole of the overland telegraph (from Adelaide to Darwin) being planted at Darwin in September 1870. The line, across 1800 miles of mostly barren wilderness, was completed in a mere 23 months and, once linked with a cable from Darwin to Java, put Australia in telegraphic communication with London.

Above: D. W. Gregory's Australian cricket team that so successfully toured England in 1878. It came as a surprise to some Englishmen that they were white: and even more of a surprise when Spofforth (left of front row) took six wickets for four runs against the M.C.C. led by W. G. Grace himself.

were beginning to monopolize the retail trades or, if they hired out their labour, were content to take their wages in opium. 'What defence can there be,' asked La Meslée philosophically, 'against people who have no respect for the law and who impose themselves on the country by their frugality, their patience, their eminently practical qualities and, in the final analysis, by the country's need of them?'

There was the rub. During the 1870s the population of Australia increased by 50 per cent but at the end of the decade there were still only three-quarters of a million immigrants in this vast continent. Australia had passed at least from childhood into adolescence – why, did not Italian companies send operas to her great cities? Had not Paris awarded prizes to her wines? Was not Britain about to ship the flower of her cricketers across the world? As La Meslée summed up the prospects: 'If a future visitor says to them, "You have done well, but you must do better still", you can be certain they will answer, "All right! God willing, we shall do whatever still needs to be done." '

China: Celestial Decay

Street groups, Kiang, China (*c.* 1870): from left to right – soup-seller, public scribe, barber and wood-burner.

'Squalor and filth are often barely concealed beneath the grand silks and embroidered dresses of the wealthy,' wrote the Revd. Alexander Williamson of the Chinese in 1870[39]. 'Opium is gnawing at the vitals of the Empire and destroying thousands of its most promising sons. . . . Falsehood and chicanery are their hope and their weapons. Scheming has been reduced to a science: deceit and lying placed upon the pedestal of ability and cleverness.'

It was not surprising that the upright and god-fearing Williamson, one of perhaps a hundred Protestant missionaries toiling in the Celestial vineyard, should have had so low an opinion of the teeming millions. He had travelled through China in the 1860s, typically with scant regard for or understanding of more than two thousand years of Confucian culture, and fortified by an unshakable conviction in the absolute superiority of the British way of life and worship. It hurt him to be patronized and patted on the shoulder 'like a dog' by Chinamen: it infuriated him that they still believed China occupied four-fifths of the world and that he came from an insignificant island on its fringe. Above all, it left him speechless that a teenage Emperor should regard himself as the mortal superior of Queen Victoria.

Yet, in Chinese eyes, it could not be otherwise. Was not the Emperor T'ung Chih, like his ancestors, God on earth, brother of the Sun, on whose countenance no common mortal could look and live, and full cousin to the Moon into the bargain? These divine presumptions apart, the earthly status of the sickly boy-Emperor was less than awe-inspiring. The fact was that since 1861, when the Emperor Hsien Feng had died leaving only one male heir of six years old, the Manchu dynasty had been in disarray.

Two regents had survived the gory intrigues that had attended the old emperor's death: his widow, because she was a homely lady and retiring by nature, and his favourite concubine Yehonala, the mother of his son, because even at twenty-six she was ruthless. Both were designated Empress Dowagers, but effective authority lay with Yehonala and (the word was) her little band of eunuchs, some of whom may or may not have felt the surgeon's knife. Her matriarchy was only temporarily interrupted in 1873 when T'ung Chih came of age, for within two years the dissipated young Emperor was awarded the happiness of a visitation of Celestial Flowers – in other words he caught smallpox, doubtless on one of his midnight forays out of the palace in search of forbidden Chinese girls – and died, childless.

This formidable lady, in contempt of all the time-honoured laws of inheritance at once set about ensuring the succession of a four-year-old from a remote branch of the fading dynasty. Having prevailed she returned triumphantly to the Regency for another fourteen years. As if the Manchu dynasty had not troubles enough without the

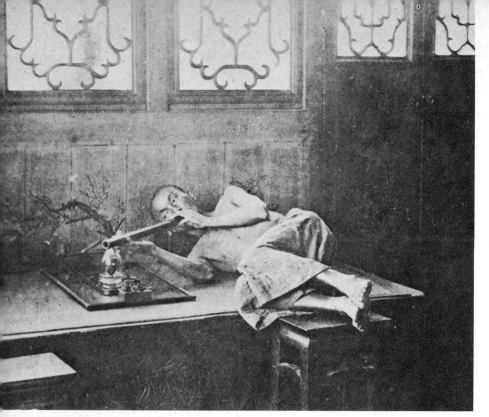

palace machinations of an ambitious woman: though established
for over two hundred years it was itself an alien régime, epitomized
still by the pigtail which all native-born Chinamen were required
to sport. The basis of its power lay in the preponderance of Manchu
officials in key posts, most of whom had long since acquired the taste
for the opium pipe, and in the once-feared platoons of Manchu
banner-men, whose dedication to their banners was not what it had
been and who had failed dismally to suppress the mushrooming
anti-Manchu secret societies. Indeed the imperial house had only
been bailed out by loyal Chinese, foreign gunboats and the exertions
of Chinese Gordon a few years earlier when faced with its most
critical threat to existence, the Taiping Rebellion.

The emergence and ultimate defeat of Taiping, the movement
which had set up and ruled its own unofficial Heavenly Kingdom
from Nanking between 1850 and 1864, proved to be of advantage
to the Western powers who had been wistfully eyeing this gigantic
market-place for so long. In the darkest hours of the rebellion (and,
let it be said, with Lord Elgin's artillery pointed at the gates of
Peking) the Manchu government had agreed to extend the meagre
trading concessions won by the foreign devils at the time of the
first Opium War.

By 1870 there were foreign missions in the Chinese capital, trading
settlements along the Yangtze as far as Hankow (although it was

Left: A Shanghai wheel-
barrow conveys a Chinese
merchant and his servant.
A commodious form of
transport (says Thomson),
capable of ferrying an
entire family.

discovered by the British traders there that the land sold them by
the Chinese was inundated by floodwaters every year), and missionaries had for several years been allowed freedom of travel into
the interior – bringing back with them, like the Revd. Williamson,
wide-eyed accounts of the sights there to be seen. Trade was brisk,
though not so brisk that the shipload of knives and forks sent by one
hopeful Sheffield cutler made any impression in the land of chopsticks.
All the same, there were a significant number of Yorkshire-made
woollens to be seen in the streets of Ningpo, Shanghai and elsewhere.

Yet the Manchu restoration – for as such was it dignified – was a
bitter disappointment. So much in the way of reform and modernization had been hoped for, but to many Government ministers
progress meant a return to true Confucian ideals. They could not
forget the pernicious quasi-Christian mumbo-jumbo put about by
the Taiping, nor forgive the foreigner for being their spiritual brother.
The Empress Dowager, cocooned in her palace and being served
with no less than a hundred different dishes at every meal, was but
a rallying-point to the forces of reaction: and these were everywhere,
the local officials, mandarins, provincial governors, the Government
itself. Railways and telegraphs, they argued, would open up the
country for the benefit of foreigners, not of the Chinese, and anyway
they would deflect the benign spirits of Fung Shui from their true
courses. So there was an end of it.

To adventurous Englishmen, revelling in the achievements of their advanced technology, this pig-headed complacency was a constant source of frustration. 'Not one Chinaman in ten thousand knows anything about the foreigner,' complained Mr Hart, chief inspector of the Chinese Customs Service. 'Not one Chinaman in a hundred thousand knows anything about foreign inventions and discoveries; and not one in a million acknowledges any superiority in either the condition or the appliances of the West.' He calculated there were perhaps twenty or thirty men in the whole of China who understood the European concept of progress, and not one of them was man enough to advocate it publicly.

Out in the distant countryside, which was Williamson's territory, increasingly through the seventies the two cultures confronted each other, the one aggressive and practical, the other defensive and suspicious. The result was the same: mutual distaste. To Williamson the universal practice of ancestor-worship was a form of idolatry 'running right in the teeth of the first Commandment' and all converts should eschew it forthwith. To the Chinese peasant it was an ancient social practice fundamental to his whole family system. A European inspecting the result of the time-honoured custom of binding a young girl's feet saw a painfully deformed foot; a Chinaman saw the shape of a sacred lily; and both knew they were right.

Below: Only a large bribe persuaded this Chinese lady (and her chaperone) to unbandage her foot (1870) – supposedly an act of gross indecency. The practice of binding a girl's feet from childhood was intended to mould them into the form of sacred lilies. The reality Thomson affirmed, had 'a very different appearance and odour'.

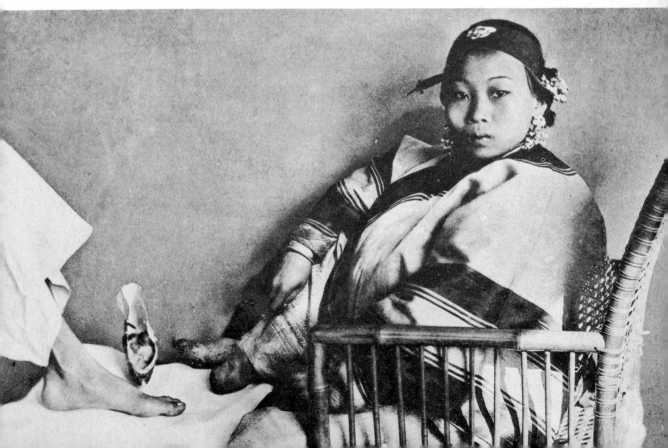

Street life in the celestial Empire in the 1870s.
Above left: A travelling grape-seller. Left: An
itinerant peep-show displaying the wonders of
the world or varying degrees of pornography
(note the unbound, clogged feet of the young
girl – showing her to be of Manchu rather than
Chinese origin). Above: The traditional method
of rolling the scented gunpowder tealeaf in tight
canvas bags, till the leaves form their
characteristic pellet shape.

How many converts Williamson made on his journeys we are not told. Few, to judge from the enthusiasm with which he describes those rare occasions when his preaching seemed to elicit anything more than 'stupid wonder'. More often, surveying a sea of upturned faces he seems to have asked himself, 'What can one feeble voice do amid these Babel sounds of ignorance and superstition?', packed up his supply of Scriptures and moved on. Of books, laboriously stowed in flimsy river-boats or loaded on to mules, he appears to have sold a great many, for the Chinese held the printed word in great awe (though whether they could read them was another matter). Undoubtedly he was a brave man. Sometimes the mute hostility of the people would turn to open menaces, even drawn knives. On such occasions he would barricade himself in his inn or – perhaps truer to modern notions of intrepid pioneers – would advance towards them 'appealing to their sense of good breeding'.

Had he been in Tientsin in the summer of 1870 he might have thought twice about so saintly an approach. In that northern city a Catholic cathedral had recently been built (tactlessly on the site of a local temple destroyed by French troops) and a mission hospital established by the Sisters of Mercy. As part of their good works they used to take waifs and strays into their orphanage and pay a small reward to those who brought them in. This developed into a racket among criminals who saw easy money to be made in kidnapping children and taking them along to the artless sisters. The discovery of this and the outbreak of an epidemic in the hospital which killed a number of the children (so giving substance to a rumour that Chinese children were being abducted and murdered so that their hearts and eyes could be used to make foreign drugs) inflamed the mob beyond restraint. It needed only the hot-tempered French consul to lose his nerve and take a pot shot at a senior mandarin for a massacre to ensue.

Ten nuns, two priests, some of their servants and the consul himself were butchered. It was by far the most tragic outburst of xenophobia of the decade, but the prejudices which were at its root were not softened one whit as time went on. A year after the massacre the English photographer John Thomson sailed past the ashes of the hospital at Tientsin and the ruins of the cathedral: he confided to his diary how repugnant to Chinese prejudices that once-noble pile must have been, standing head and shoulders above all other buildings in the city (it was in fact forbidden for any building in China to exceed the height of the roofs of the Imperial Palace – on the grounds that the owner must therefore consider himself superior to the Emperor). He also quotes a pamphlet that urged the utter extermination of foreigners, perpetuating the same superstitions that had underlain the Tientsin catastrophe. Silver, claimed this bizarre pamphlet, could be obtained 'by compounding lead with the eyes

The abbot and monks of Fushan monastery, 1870. Thomson noted the resemblance of the Buddhist attire to the monastic dress of ancient Europe, and remarked on the civilised nature of their rules ('Thou shalt not smack in eating' amongst others).

of Chinamen', adding that the eyes of foreigners were of no use for this amazing alchemy!

Thomson's account of the Chinese, published in 1875[30], is more objective than Williamson's, if only because he went in the role of observer rather than evangelist. He experienced quite as many ordeals as Williamson and as much open hostility, for his cumbersome photographic equipment was as self-evidently diabolic to a Chinaman as the missionary's sermons. Taking a portrait was a touchy business: many believed that the very act robbed a man's body of part of its vital principle and that death was sure to follow. The best the hapless photographer could hope for at times was that 'the unfortunates would fall down on bended knees and beseech me not to take their likeness or their life with the fatal lens . . .' At other times he himself barely escaped the vengeance of the mob with his tripod and his life.

For all that, the picture of everyday life in China that he brought back was largely sympathetic and free from the moral sententiousness which infused so many of his contemporaries. His curiosity took him everywhere his British passport allowed, from the houses of the Peking upper class, where to his astonishment he observed photographic and electrical experiments being conducted, to the hovels of Amoy, where female infanticide was as much the rule as the exception, so dire was the poverty. He could not walk past a grogshop without peering in to examine its battered, bulldog customers, nor visit a

Right: A Hong Kong artist at work in 1870, enlarging and reproducing in paint photographic portraits – largely for the benefit of foreign sailors.

Left: A petty criminal condemned to the punishment of the wooden collar. His offence is writ large on the collar, his fate to depend on the charity of passers-by for food.

tea factory without describing in detail the coolies tossing balls of tealeaves about with their feet (to produce the shape of the curious gunpowder leaf). He sees, in countless Cantonese shops, the notice 'Schroffing taught here'. He learns that schroffers are coiners of spurious dollars, and that to conduct business in Canton you must be at least as wily as they are. The pawnshops, he notes, are the most prosperous establishments in the street, as heavily guarded as banks.

Beggars infest his route, a caste of their own with a hierarchy as rigid as a civil service, 'revolting, diseased and filthy objects' with refinements of deformity that gag the imagination – but which quite often are assumed each morning like a uniform! They do not steal, for they do not have to: those who do are the lowest dregs of society, and sooner or later will be caught and strung up by their thumbs until the arms are out of joint and the bare bone exposed. To catch thieves is the job of the *Ma-qui*, but he is more of a broker in reality who will accept a percentage from both robbed and robber, and thus restore the status quo in civilized fashion. It is the thief who will not accept his terms who gets strung up – and in that case the *Ma-qui* too is liable to be whipped. 'He then whips his subordinates, and they in turn whip the thieves. Should this plan fail,' reports Thomson, 'it is reported that the police have been whipped and the stolen property cannot be found.'

The arsenal at Nanking, 1871. One of China's few concessions to foreign influence after the 'restoration' was to inaugurate an armaments programme on Western lines – to recover some of the military ground lost since the Chinese invention of the gun in the thirteenth century.

Gambling, he observes, is the incorrigible vice of the Chinese, accounting for the petty pilfering he endured throughout his travels and for the affluence of the pawnbrokers. In Hong Kong – where the British had been in possession for nearly thirty years – some attempt was made to license it, to no effect whatsoever. It contributed some 14,000 Hong Kong dollars a month to the treasury, but the governors of the colony were so embarrassed by possession of this tainted money that they preferred to drop it into the sea rather than do anything constructive with it. The licensing scheme was abandoned after three months, while in China the gambling dens continued unmolested by officials, possibly because there was a far greater national vice to exercise their attention.

Williamson had been publishing no less than the literal truth when he complained that opium was gnawing at the vitals of the

Empire. Ever since the East India Company had begun exploiting the commercial possibilities of the poppy in the eighteenth century, the opium traffic into China had increased inexorably, so that by the 1870s it had percolated to every stratum of society. In Canton alone there were more than five hundred shops where the drug could be bought; in every city in the country even children could be seen smoking it in the streets; uncounted millions were helpless addicts. It enslaved, as Thomson noted, every estate, from the miserable boatmen of the Yangtsze who huddled together in the holds of their boat smoking themselves into merciful sleep, to the richly-embroidered merchants on their opium couches, surrounded by all the paraphernalia of sophisticated inhalation, 'with girls in constant attendance, some ready to prepare and charge the bowl of the pipe with opium and others to sing sweet melodies to waft the sleeper off into dreamland.'

Periodically in the past the Government had made token efforts to curtail the trade, all doomed to early failure – largely through the addiction of those detailed to enforce the imperial edicts. The size of the problem was overwhelming: to extinguish smuggling was obviously impossible, and to punish offenders, as one laconic governor put it, would require that they be lined up along the roads, for the gaols certainly could not accommodate them.

To Thomson, even as he marvelled at the decrepit magnificence of this mysterious kingdom and at the patient intricacy of its craftsmen, it was as if the land lay in a drugged sleep. Not just under the anaesthetic of foreign opium, but in terms of its almost wilful policy of stagnation. In response to the fierce impact of the West in the nineteenth century China had turned back in on itself. It countered new teaching with old superstitions (one popular one was that some race beyond the Chinese pale had holes above their hearts so that they could be carried along on poles, like spitted herrings), and it reacted to new weapons with half-hearted attempts at arsenals where the shells manufactured 'turned out much more deadly projectiles in the hands of their own men than they could ever have proved in the ranks of the enemy.' Anyway, it was Thomson's opinion that the rulers 'with blind pride are arming a beggarly soldiery to fight for nothing that is worth defending.'

Perhaps it was not in the nature of an English gentleman to overestimate foreigners (any more than it was a Chinaman's) but even as he wrote those words the imperialist powers were nibbling away, almost unopposed, at China's satellites: Britain in Burma, France in Vietnam, Russia in the north, and, worst of all, Japan in Korea. For in Japan, another country where a sub-medieval gloom had lain over the cities for centuries, a truly amazing transformation had taken place which could have been an inspiration to the Celestial Empire instead of a deadly threat.

Japan:The Rising Sun

East meet West: a fraternization unthinkable before the Meiji Restoration.

'Madame, I must ask you for the recipe for the salad we have eaten this evening. I take it it is your own creation.'

'The Japanese salad?'

'It is Japanese?'

'I call it that.'

'Why?'

'Because it must have a name, and everything's Japanese nowadays.'

So ran the polite table-talk in one of Alexandre Dumas' novels in the mid-1880s, though if it gives the impression that the French enthusiasm for *Japonisme* was just a passing fancy, that would be mistaken. Ever since the Paris World Fair of 1867 had 'introduced' Japanese art to the West – and Manet's portrait of Zola the same year had, as it were, set an aesthetic stamp of approval on it – French society had pursued this exotic fashion with something like scholarly dedication. Many other artists came under its influence, notably Degas and Monet; earnest little magazines devoted to its study were circulated; smart shops in the Rue de Rivoli and elsewhere were given over to the sale of fragile oriental fans, paper-thin porcelain and delicate prints; exclusive societies were formed to eat Japanese food on the floor and talk hungrily about Japanese art.

The passion and the curiosity spread to England, to Whistler, who even began to sign his work with a butterfly device like a Japanese seal, and to the furniture designers (who were slightly perplexed how to reconcile their dainty prototypes with the somewhat bulkier British anatomy). You could walk down to Albert Gate in London and inspect a Japanese village built by Japanese workmen and manned by Japanese attendants: or you could take a carriage to the Savoy and laugh at the antics of the Mikado and his court – which at the same time drew howls of protest from the Japanese consul.

But while this flowering of the East in Europe was a fascinating interlude in Paris or London, the rapid unfolding to Japanese eyes, as the 1870s progressed, of the mysteries of the West was a revelation. Until 1868 Japan had existed for more than two centuries in total self-imposed isolation from the outside world. On pain of death no Japanese could travel abroad, any more than foreign barbarians could set foot on Japanese soil (except for a handful of Dutchmen in an island off Nagasaki). Time meant nothing, dignified ceremony everything – from the way you sipped your tea to the way you disembowelled yourself before honourable suicide.

A feudal miasma had settled over the land, like a fog over ornamental gardens. In Kyoto the Mikado *reigned*, a moral and spiritual force but politically impotent, while in Yedo (Tokyo) the Shogun *ruled*, as a powerful and military governor. Throughout the countryside the provincial lords were held in more or less firm allegiance,

A Japanese officer in full mask and panoply, 1870 – medieval splendour destined shortly to give way to Prussian uniforms and efficiency.

Overleaf: The Shogun's private bathing-place on the Tokaido Hasa, one of the main imperial roads linking the major cities of Japan.

though with autocratic control over their own territories and jealousy protected by their retinues of samurai. The peasants as ever, generation on generation, tended their paddy-fields and prostrated themselves in the path of their lords. In peace and insularity, art, crafts and traditional beliefs flourished; but outside the world was growing up.

The first serious intrusion of the world had come in 1853, with the arrival of the American, Commander Perry, in Tokyo Bay, with four warships and a demand for trading rights. Perry was not a man to be denied, nor was the governor of Uraga, with his wobbly junks and clumsy broadswords, in a position to deny him. The rulers of Japan were split between the die-hard conservatives, who were for driving the foreigner back into the sea at any price, and the progressives, who looked at Perry's gift of a telegraph (and at the peasants who stared for hours at the wire waiting to catch a message going by) and realized that sooner or later Japan must bow to the inevitable. The amiable view prevailed, but in the years that followed, as more and more diplomats, traders and itinerant seamen jostled into the one foreign concession at Yokohama, the anti-foreign factions continued to nurture their hatred, so that sudden death in the night became an ever-present threat for those vulnerable Western pioneers.

In 1868, all this changed dramatically. For some years great underground opposition had been growing to the Shogun and his Tokugawa clan – from those who despised his weakness towards foreigners, from those who were suffering an erosion of their standard of living in the frozen economy, from those who simply resented the Tokugawas. In 1867, a figurehead had emerged from the fossilized imperial house to bring together these loose coalitions, the new 16-year-old Mikado, Mutsuhito. In particular around him were gathered the powerful western clans from Satsuma, Choshu, Tosa and Hizen.

Sporadic outbreaks of rebellion and a recognizable defeat in February 1868 proved enough to persuade the young Shogun (not much older than Mutsuhito) to resign his authority in April, although a number of obdurate samurai held out in their medieval castles against imperial forces for a few more months. But by the beginning of 1869 the group around the Meiji Emperor (to give him his reign title) felt secure enough to mark the New Era with a flurry of decrees. Feudalism was abolished and the provincial lords were persuaded to return 'heaven and earth' to the Emperor (to whom they rightfully belonged anyway); and in due course a land tax was introduced to take the place of feudal dues, and conscription to create an army free from feudal loyalties. And to emphasize just how democratic things could get, the Emperor himself decreed that henceforth his Divine Presence could be displayed to mere mortals, even to foreigners.

One of the first Englishmen to witness this epoch-making manifestation was Algernon Mitford, one of the new British legation staff

in Tokyo. As he gazed upon this brocaded young man, eyebrows shaved, cheeks rouged and teeth blackened, the significance of the occasion bore down upon him (he recalled many years later): 'Now, suddenly, the veil of the temple had been rent and the Boy-God, in defence of whose Divinity myriads of his subjects were ready gladly to lay down their lives, had descended from the clouds to take his place among the children of men, and not only that, but he had actually allowed his sacred face to be seen and had held communion with the Beasts from Without.' But, of course, the beasts from without were now rather more acceptable within. In the interval between Perry's arrival and the Meiji 'restoration' there had been ample opportunity to observe some of the wonders these westerners had brought with them, their steamships and firearms, photographic machines and newspapers, their cigarettes and brass bands. A few adventurous souls had even been permitted to sail into the unknown, and had returned with fairy-tale stories of buildings more than two storeys high, of iron roads that spanned continents, and armies that moved as one man. To some Japanese, who had known only handcarts and suits of armour, their inferiority was a matter of shame; to others it was clear that Japan's only defence against the foreigner was to learn all his secrets, in as short a space of time as possible.

Kobe and Osaka had been opened to foreign trade in 1868. The following year Tokyo was permitted to foreign residents and the western legations moved there en masse. The government publicly revoked its anti-western slogans and recorded its intention to look henceforth to other countries for help in making up for centuries of lost progress. Meanwhile women should stop blacking their teeth and gentlemen were advised to renounce their topknots (this caused much unrest among barbers until they saw there was as much work in a short head of hair; very soon the weirdest signboards were announcing their willingness to have a go at western coiffure: 'Barber to Shave Beard or to Dress Hairs Way').

This official government pronouncement opened the floodgates, and revealed in the Japanese character that desire to tackle anything with an intensity that is both admirable and alarming. With the whole world at their disposal to find models for the new enlightenment, they duly sallied forth, solemnly inspected and made their decision. Tokyo Central station was to be based upon that in Amsterdam, the Museum was to be the offspring of South Kensington in London, the Government building for the new northern capital at Sapporo was to be . . . well, naturally, the spitting image of the Capitol in Washington. Nothing but the best would do, and that meant looking to the British Navy and the Prussian Army for inspiration. In due course, when time allowed for the formulation of a civil code and a universal educational system, you would have discerned (at the very least) British, American, French and German particles coming to-

Faithful pupils: Japanese army officers with their French instructors and newly-tailored French uniforms. Following German successes in the Franco-Prussian war of 1870, these were summarily replaced by German instructors (and, of course, German uniforms).

gether to make up these strange atoms.

Sometimes the innovations were misplaced and short-sighted. Westerners may have welcomed the advent of glass and brick in place of those draughty paper partitions which appeared to slide in every direction (so that visitors seemed to enter a room at whichever point was most convenient), but it was to prove a crop from which the earthquakes would later reap a bitter harvest. More often, though, the results were simply eccentric. At an early stage the Mikado decided that frockcoat, pinstripe trousers and spats were the epitome of polite western dress. No doubt his own wardrobe was from Savile Row, but the sartorial efforts of his more slavish subjects verged on the preposterous. Christopher Dresser, the designer who helped to import some western curiosities to Tokyo Museum in 1877, was much saddened by the efforts of one Japanese dandy[9].

He wore mittens and the sleeves of his coat were at least six inches too long, hence it was only by a judicious arrangement of fold, and by keeping his elbows somewhat akimbo, that the mittens, which were evidently articles of clothing not to be hidden from view, were kept visible. The legs of his trousers were as much too long as the sleeves of his coat; while his hat, which was much too large for his head, was kept in its place by a handkerchief rolled into the form of a ball and carefully placed between his forehead and the rim. . . . It is a truly pitiable sight to see fine men arrayed in our miserable dress, and that looking its worst, when the native costume is so graceful and lends great dignity to the wearer.

Likewise Dresser was disappointed to find himself served with Crosse and Blackwell's potted meats and Keiller's Dundee marmalade at his hotel – though when he did come face-to-face with homespun Japanese food, sea-slugs, sake and seaweed, he admitted to second thoughts. He is confronted with 'a putty-like compound with green exterior, but in attempting to bite a piece from the mass I encounter a serious difficulty. . . . I find I am drawing out an attenuated string of the ductile dainty, and that the portion in my mouth is still connected with the larger mass now resting on the floor. I verily believe that one mass of such food could be drawn into a thread which would span the Pacific itself: at last, in my agony, I swallow the mass, but even then it seems an age before I can break the thread which binds me to the dish on the floor.' But this is nothing to the discomfort to be suffered at the next course, which turns out to be raw slices of flesh cut from

Hakoni village, 1870. A typical Japanese village street, guarded by a Sekisho (or barrier-gate). Anyone passing through was obliged to lift his hat, to enable the guard to scrutinise his face.

Overleaf: The beautiful
Mayonashi Valley, a day's
ride out of Yokohama.
Note the open-air bath-tub
session in progress (bottom
left), a harmless pastime
unaccountably to be
outlawed by imperial
decree.

a living fish! A 'refinement of barbaric cruelty' which he finds hard
to reconcile with the geniality and loving nature of the Japanese.
But then, he reminds himself, how could there be any self-reproach
among a people more than seventy of whom had committed hara-
kiri a few weeks earlier for their part in a local rebellion?

But whatever inhibitions the westerner entertained about succumb-
ing to native custom, the Japanese rapidly shook off any they might
have had about their new lifestyle. The native quarter of Yokohama
was illuminated with gas lamps long before the foreign settlement
got round to it (partly because the different nationalities could not
agree about paying the gas rate). The better-off could be seen strolling
along these radiant streets with brollies over their arm or bowling
along them in the fashionable new jinrikishas – perhaps up to the new
railway station (after 1877) for a spin up to Kyoto in the new steam

On the road from Yedo to Osaka, 1868, photographed by Beato, who describes it as a major road flanked by pines (to shade the Daimios and their retinues, who frequently travelled along it to the Shogun's capital, Yedo).

engine, where the ticket-collectors wore peaked caps, just like on the Great Western. The world was new, the world was fast, the world – as one new Japanese journalist lyricized on a new newspaper – was 'so jolly!'

And into this jolly little world, as the 1870s matured, crowded all manner of artists, engineers, teachers (any adventurer who responded to the Japanese advertisements for 'professors' considered himself entitled to be called one) – and missionaries. Before 1873 any members of this ubiquitous breed who succeeded in setting up their stalls in Japan had had to do so in the utmost secrecy, for the traditional horror of Christianity rooted in centuries had alone survived the Meiji's revolution. Only when it dawned on the country's leaders that the nations of the West were decidedly not going to look kindly on trade with a people who, in theory anyway, persecuted Christians, did they reluctantly open the sluices to the waiting flood of evangelists.

Many of the other foreigners did not welcome this influx of propaganda. Some who had been in the country long enough to learn to respect the transcendent calm of the Shinto temples and the ageless grandeur of the Buddhist shrines felt, like many Japanese, that the new religion would ultimately undermine a profound culture, as its tight-lipped moralists had already persuaded the authorities to ban such vicious pastimes as open-air tub-washing on one's doorstep. And indeed there was a beefiness about so many of the missionaries which grated on the sensibilities, as Christopher Dresser discovered one day when the Mikado passed by in the street.

One English missionary . . . availed himself of a step to make himself conspicuous, and nodding his head defiantly, declared audibly that he would not acknowledge the heathen sovereign. Although not of a combative disposition, I felt almost irresistibly impelled to give that missionary a lesson in manners such as he would not easily forget. . . . If this is the manner in which our missionaries act (and I confess that while in Japan I saw little to admire, but much to condemn, in those with whom I came in contact), we cannot wonder at illiterate men acting in defiance of right and order.

As it turned out the crusades of the seventies and eighties had little long-term influence on the 'essentially unspeculative' minds of the Japanese: the unintelligible catechisms proved to make far less impression than the sweeping social advances of the same period, and faltered in the end in the face of the nation's growing self-confidence. The time was shortly to come when Japan could dispense with her western crutches (and the strange contortions she adopted in employing them), and emerge as a world power capable of humbling both China and Russia within a few years of each other. To those Japanese who had toiled to extricate themselves from the stagnation of centuries perhaps it had been a painfully slow process: for those westerners who had once looked wistfully to Japan as an antidote to creeping industrial revolution, it seemed the rising sun had risen with dizzying speed.

India: Noon of Empire

Up-country: the planter's bungalow, family and household.

In spite of the very best efforts of the Orient and Peninsular Company, their salt-water baths and unending supply of ice and soda, the three-week passage to India was a trying business. In the tropics the steam punkahs provided in the better class of cabin were scarcely able to restrain the apoplexy; in bad weather the delights of the steamship's vaunted à la carte palled before the retching of one's companions. And what companions! mused Mr Monier Williams, Professor of Sanskrit at Oxford University, returning in 1875 to the India of his childhood[41]. 'Sundry male oddities – long-bearded, short-bearded and beardless, wived and wifeless – divers eccentric, husbandless females of uncertain ages and vague antecedants, a few solitary wives on the way to join their husbands, one or two flirting bachelors, a bevy of pretty unmarried girls . . . and a residium of unsortable nondescripts.' Still, things were better than in his youth. At least the ships now had portholes and the new canal at Suez had done away with that caravan across the desert from Cairo to the Red Sea.

And how reassuring Bombay was at the end of it all: the elegant expanse of the Esplanade, the shaded park, a cricket match and scattered applause, soda water and brandy bottles peeping out of ice pails. You could almost imagine yourself back in the Parks at Oxford . . . well not quite, perhaps. Just beyond were the teeming alleyways, the disconcerting noiseless footfalls of an unshod multitude, reeking hovels and importunate holy men. 'With the Hindoos holiness and dirtiness are almost synonymous, and certainly these are the worst-washed men I ever saw,' remarked another new arrival in Bombay, Mr Drew Gay of the *Daily Telegraph*[16]. 'I should say at a rough guess that the holiness on that man was a quarter of an inch thick.' The Anglo-Indians could build their fashionable suburbs out of town, keep their own clubs and railway compartments, retire to the exclusive coolness of their own hill-stations, but they could never create anything more than the illusion that this was Home. India was for ever lurking there, at once a responsibility and a threat. If you were stupid enough, or arrogant enough, you could shut your eyes to it. An enraged correspondent to a Calcutta newspaper, alarmed at moves to give native magistrates wider powers, might splutter: 'The only people who have a right to India are the British. The *so-called* Indians have no right whatsoever.' But India in the 1870s was very much less than a generation away from the Mutiny; many Anglo-Indians had witnessed the senseless brutality of Meerut and Lucknow or vividly recalled the carnage at Cawnpore. The bitterness and lust for revenge were gone now, but the Mutiny had profoundly altered the course of British imperialism and therefore the everyday lives of its white representatives.

John Company (as the East India Company was known) with its private armies and privileges, had disappeared and a new breed of administrator was being shipped over from England, in yearly larger batches. Competition-wallahs, the old India hands contemptuously called them, after the examination they now had to pass before going East. The established families with a long tradition of service in India resented these usurpers, as well they might in many cases, for they brought with them the bureaucrat's consciousness of superiority that is as impregnable as any caste system. 'An advanced native, of independent character, once complained to me,' even Monier Williams was bound to admit, 'that most Englishmen appeared to him to walk about the world with an air as if God Almighty intended the whole universe to be English. He probably had been thrown with young civilians recently imported from England. Few others would think of lording it over their Indian brethren in any offensive manner.'

The professor is to be doubted on that score. There was many a planter, outside the effective range of the administration, who ruled his far-flung empire like a feudal lord – but, as the dramatic inroads Assam tea was making into the Chinese monopoly showed, at least he was materially benefitting the country. The competition-wallah could point to no significant increase in Civil Service efficiency or rationalization of that hydra-like machine which could reproduce bits of official paper indefinitely. The standing joke up at Simla was that Indian government was a despotism of despatch-boxes, tempered by the loss of the keys.

The demeanour of the new administrators was especially unfortunate in view of the authorities' determination to learn from the mistakes of the Mutiny – which above all had demonstrated the total lack of contact between the two communities. Indians were now eligible to sit for the Civil Service exam (though none succeeded in passing for the first ten years) and as education increased – in 1873 there were nearly a million children in primary schools – so the educated Indian began to fill more and more authoritative posts, in the law courts, the police, the public services. The more reactionary Anglo-Indians watched this with mounting disquiet: the *Babus* would take over, not by mutiny this time, but by modernization.

The underlying fear was of reform, not of material progress. The Anglo-Indian of the seventies was quite prepared to throw himself heart and soul into the construction of public works, railways, irrigation projects and great municipal buildings. Indeed few eras have witnessed a more fanciful flowering of megalomanic architecture, from the Decorated Marzipan of Bombay Station to the Byzantine Neo-Gothic of the Municipal Hall or the Scotch-Hydro of the Viceroy's summer palace at Simla. The natives understood and appreciated such civic munificence: 'Next morning I started, in company with Mr Arthur Crawford, several years the Municipal Commissioner of Bombay, to look at the Grand Bombay Markets which were erected

An Anglo-Indian luxuriates in his palanquin.

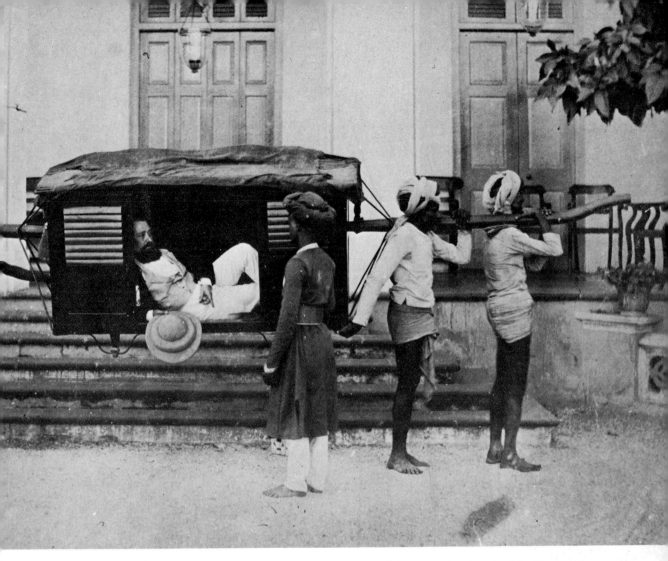

by him, and are still called by his name,' records Mr Drew Gay.
'A somewhat lengthy drive brought us to the outside of the building,
a large and stately edifice. . . On the outside was the name of Arthur
Crawford writ large; and no sooner did the good people of the market
descry their benefactor than, with great show of respect and even
affection, they made a path for him through the hundreds of buyers
who were already at their stalls.'

But the gulf between benevolent responsibility and actually *caring*
was exposed most painfully by the devastating famine in Southern
India in 1877. That year an unusually severe drought, abetted by the
annual visitation of cholera, claimed up to six million lives (so some
officials calculated) in the huge and helpless tracts between Bombay
and the south of the Madras Presidency. It drove parents to abandon
their children and struggle northwards in the hope of eking out their

lives. It became a tragically common sight in the streets of Madras to see gaunt and fleshless children, barely ten years old, wandering aimlessly through the city and cradling an even more hopeless bundle of humanity in their arms.

'Men and women, old and young, even cripples, mothers with infants on their hips and naked children', reported Monier Williams from Madras, 'were earnestly engaged in gleaning up every grain that escaped from the sacks on the piers and on the shore. Many were provided with coarse sieves, by means of which a few rice grains were, with infinite pains, separated from the bushels of sand. On the pier every crevice was searched, and every discoloured grain eagerly scraped up, mixed as it was with dirt, ejected betel-juice and filth of all kinds.' The horror of it quickly impressed itself on the Government: funds were opened in London and generously subscribed, grain ships were speedily despatched from the north, and civil servants willingly sweated out the crisis in the furnace of plains to try and cope, instead of retiring to the hills.

But for all that patent philanthropy, '*We do not care for the people of India*,' Florence Nightingale felt obliged to write in 1878[22]. 'Do we even care enough to know about their daily lives of lingering death from causes which we could so well remove? We have taken their lands and their rule and their rulers into our charge for State reasons

Below: The last of the herd. The sufferings of the 1877/8 Madras famine, observed by W. W. Hooper, have a tragically familiar look to them even today.

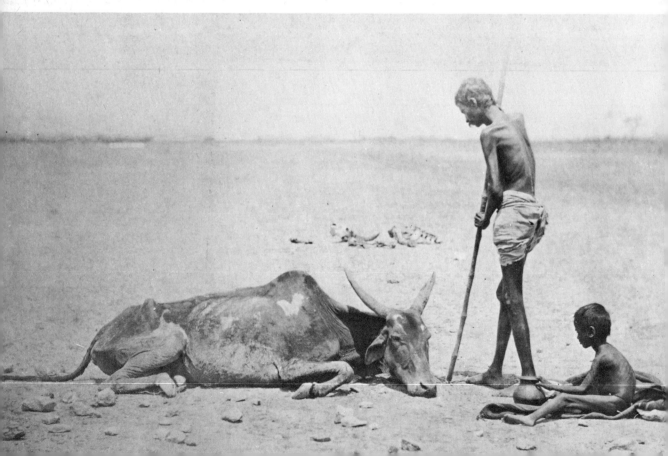

Above: Well-to-do Parsees in Bombay, posing *en famille*, 1867.

of our own. . . But for them themselves – these patient, silent, toiling millions of India who scarcely but for suffering know their right hand from their left – for their daily lives and deaths we do *not* as a nation practically care. Have we no voice for these voiceless millions?'

Anglo-Indians tended, sometimes with good cause, to suspect the motives behind the flood of liberal and humanitarian sentiments that issued from the mother country. But here Florence Nightingale touched a nerve. After all, though the distress of 1877 was by far the most widespread, it was no less than the fourth major famine in ten years and little had been done in many parts of India to anticipate or prevent such catastrophes. The peasant on his *ryot* – land rented from the government – was encouraged to grow cotton, because you couldn't eat cotton. And if his arid plot did not produce sufficient to pay the rent and the vicious tax on salt, to keep his family in a meagre ration of coarse rice and *dhall*, and to keep him from the money-lender, well what else could you expect? 'The saddest sight to be seen', concluded Miss Nightingale, 'is the peasant in our own Eastern Empire. But we do not look at this sight.'

Indeed the Anglo-Indian did not even look much at the procession of Rajahs, Maharajahs, Nizams and Guicowars which paraded in and out of his existence, especially at the interminable receptions which, since the native princes had been restored to imperial favour for their 'loyalty' during the Mutiny, had grown ever more formal.

The sacred city of Benares,
1875.

On the occasion of the Prince of Wales' official visit in 1876 Drew Gay of the *Telegraph* had the opportunity to inspect these curious personages at close hand: gnarled, olive-brown old gentlemen bowed down beneath of their ludicrous turbans, as broad as umbrellas, and solemn little specimens like the Guicowar of Baroda, nine years old and encrusted from head to toe with jewels.

If he of Mysore is radiant with jewels this royal seedling from Baroda is more magnificent still. On his neck and breast, his turban and his very shoes, everywhere glisten diamonds, emeralds, rubies and pearls. He is well aware of his own importance; and though not so old as his Mysore rival, acts his part well. And when the chairs are brought and the two sit down each eyes the other with great curiosity – perhaps also mentally placing a valuation on the others jewels – and then each turns his head away with an expression very like contempt.

The extreme youth of much of India's nobility presented many headaches for the civil servants when the time came for the ritual exchange of presents. 'One very irreverent person suggested that a handsome whistle, a top and a box of the best building bricks would have been most suitable; but he was very properly suppressed.' In the event, one suspects, the final choices – snuff-boxes and English picture books – must have been as welcome as the suits of armour the

Loyalty rewarded: for their non-involvement in the Mutiny of 1857 most native princes were permitted to maintain – even augment – their lavish life-styles, their retinues and royal barges. But like the jewel-encrusted Maharaja Holkar of Indore (right), photographed in 1877, their presence was rather more decorative then functional.

On 1 January 1877 Queen Victoria, seated (left) on the ivory throne presented to her by the Rajah of Travar, was proclaimed Empress of India. The Proclamation was made at Delhi (right) with due pomp and ceremony by the Viceroy Lord Lytton (from the Canopy, left centre) flanked by separate amphitheatres for Europeans and native princes.

princelings hoped the Prince of Wales to be in urgent need of.

The urge to identify the native rulers with the British Crown sometimes produced odd results. When in 1876 Queen Victoria acceded to the whim of Disraeli that she should assume the title Empress of India, it was decided that the good news be imparted to India at a splendid Proclamation in Delhi the following January. In the meantime the Viceroy, Lord Lytton, entered into the spirit of things and ordered that each prince should be equipped with a proper coat-of-arms and family motto: the brand-new escutcheons, when they arrived, turned out to be far beyond the strength of one strong man. Nevertheless the princes responded with admirable patriotism by importing mechanical organs that churned out 'God Save The Queen', or by teaching their bandmasters to play 'God Bless The Prince Of Wales' on the bagpipes.

But if the Indians' efforts to compromise politely with the mores of their British masters bordered often on the bizarre, there was no reciprocal attempt made by the Anglo-Indians. By the 1870s their hierarchies had achieved an inflexibility daunting even to well-prepared Englishmen, and their patterns of life settled into an invincible routine which a novice memsahib departed from at her peril: *chota hazri*, or tea-and-toast, at break of day, brandy-pawnees at bedtime, and Mulligatawny soup for Sunday lunch. Even their jargon seemed designed to reinforce the self-conscious isolation,

Above: Often far from the reach of government, tea-planters ruled their little empires much as they pleased.

with their tiffins, and jutkas, and *dhobi-wallahs*. In 1871 a set of satires called *The Chutney Lyrics* appeared anonymously in Madras, one of them being an Anglo-Indian version of 'Come Into The Garden, Maud':

> She is coming, my godown, my ghaut!
>   She is coming, my dawk, my sweet!
> My cutcherry leaps, and my tope
>   In my bosom begins to beat —
> O my love, my massoolah, my ghee,
>   Thy poochie is at thy feet!

But how many saw the joke?

There were social pitfalls at every step for the unwary, from getting the precedence of your guests wrong at dinner to choosing the wrong hill-station. These resorts, where white folk unfailingly repaired in an Indian summer, were carefully graded. A humble Collector would no more be seen at Simla ('the portals of heaven') or even Ootacamund in the Nilgiri Hills ('snooty Ooty') than the Viceroy would think of putting up at Darjeeling for the season. The annual exodus to one of these havens could be as formidable as an overland safari. To get to Simla, Drew Gay advises,

Below: The Prince of Wales, during his royal visit of 1875, poses with the trophies of a day's tiger-shooting in Jaipur. Overleaf: Bears, too, often found themselves hopelessly outnumbered.

You must needs submit to a five hours' journey in that most uncomfortable of vehicles, the dak-gharry – a kind of dilapidated London cab with the well boarded over – and then a perpetual ascent upon ledges more or less narrow for fifty-six miles further, your choice of conveyance lying between a kind of palanquin, called in the language of the district a 'jhampan', borne on the unequal shoulders of eight reckless savages, or a country pony the only qualification of which is that he is tolerably sure-footed.

But then there were one's own effects to transport. For a family of four a train of a dozen camels was recommended, though if you were taking your piano you'd need to supplement that with fourteen to sixteen coolies. Once there, however, among the towering rhododendron bushes, there was the giddying round of tennis and tea-parties, whist and amateur theatricals – and (as *Vanity Fair* added) 'picnics and adultery'. For in the hill-stations, if nowhere else in India, there would be an abundance of women, summer widows through the exigencies of their husbands' duties, bored and bitchy in spite of the cooling mountain airs. It was said of Simla that you could not sleep at night for the noise of the grinding of axes.

Subalterns straying incautiously into such society were fair game: 'I know a station', claimed Drew Gay, 'in which five officers in one English regiment have been inveigled into the joys and sorrows of matrimony by thoughtful mammas, during the past six months.'

The Second Afghan War, 1879, was a classic example of a British punitive expedition (to avenge the murder of the legation at Kabul). The Indian army (below: a detachment of Rattray's Sikhs guarding prisoners) under General Roberts (right: inspecting captured cannon) made short, sharp work of the miscreant mountain tribes.

Such were the perils of peacetime, and it doubtless came as some relief in 1878 for the army to learn that Britain's crescendo of Russophobia had reached the pitch of demanding an invasion of Afghanistan to ensure that country's 'neutrality'. For years Russia had been pressing inexorably southwards eating up the barbarous tribes of Central Asia – no great loss to the world, but when Russian armies stood on the borders of Afghanistan, the gateway to India, and the keys of that gate were in the custody of an unreliable scoundrel like Sher Ali, the time had come to act.

For three years the Indian army, under General Roberts, was actively engaged in the mountains of Afghanistan, first in deposing Sher Ali and establishing a British Mission in Kabul, then in avenging the appalling massacre of that Mission in 1879. In April 1881 the whole expedition was withdrawn to India having, in practical terms, achieved little more than an expensive show of force, but with the comfortable feeling that the integrity of the Queen's empire and a civilized way of life has been safeguarded for a while longer. The officers returned to their pig-sticking, tent-pegging, hunting with the hounds, snooker (an invention of Anglo-India comparable to the curries of the Madras Club), and the rowdier pastimes of the mess. And up in the hills 'the ringing laughter from the Badminton court mingled with the music from the Institute, the clicking of billiard balls, and the soft conversation of lovers.'

Africa: Tourists, Travellers & Colonisers

Opening ceremony for the Suez Canal: Port Said, 1869.

On the evening of 17 November 1869 in the brand-new city of Ismailia, mid-way between the Mediterranean and the Red Sea, a truly regal banquet was in progress. The reflections of ten thousand lanterns scintillated in the placid waters of Lake Timsah, strains of the Blue Danube filtered out into the endless desert behind, and fireworks lit up the sky. The Austrian Emperor, the Empress Eugénie, the Crown Prince of Prussia and other assorted royalty were seated at a stupendous dinner, their appetites sharpened no doubt by the twelve-hour voyage from Port Said down one of the wonders of modern engineering, the new Suez Canal.

Not everything had augured well for this glittering opening: Verdi had failed to turn in his masterpiece commissioned for the inauguration of Cairo Opera House, Port Said had been nearly razed to the ground by an exploding warehouse of fireworks, and at the eleventh hour a police launch had run aground in the Canal, blocking it completely. But now, surveying his new city of bars, boulevards and estaminets to which he had graciously donated his name and beaming benignly at this glittering throng, Ismail, Khedive of Egypt, could be well pleased with himself. The African Paris someone had called it, and yet it was nothing to the glories of new Cairo with its arcades and palaces, theatre and opera houses. Soon Egypt, and its whiskered Khedive, could worthily take its place beside the great states of Europe.

Yet Ismail's enthusiasm for the Canal was by no means universally shared. Even in France, which had provided the technology and much of the money, there were uneasy voices. The new isthmus would become a battlefield, Ernest Renan prophetically told de Lesseps. 'A single Bosphorus has hitherto sufficed for the troubles of the world; you have created a second and much more important one.' In Britain in particular the whole project, and France's growing influence in Egypt, was viewed with hearty disapproval. *Punch*, updating the riddle of the sphinx, wondered what would come of

> This pot-pourri of East and West,
> Pillau and potage à la bisque;
> Circassian belles whom Worth has dressed,
> And Parisiennes à l'odalisque?

To the British politician Africa was a savage and unsalubrious continent: his interest in it, if any, was strictly confined to those fringes where trade might profitably be conducted, his knowledge of the interior little better than Herodotus'. Until recently it had been a place for adventurers like Burton, Speke and Livingstone. Now the crowned heads of Europe were actually enduring to set foot on it. And tourists! So William Russell noted vexatiously in his diary[24].

These stirrings of sophistication on the Lower Nile were drawing even Mr Thomas Cook's tourists there in droves. 'They fill hotels inconveniently,' grumbled Russell, 'they crowd sites which ought to be approached in reverential silence with a noisy crowd, and they do not tend to inspire the natives with a sentiment of respect for our people. The very higgling and bargaining which accompany their ways makes one feel very uncomfortable. . . Mr Monpensier Brown and Miss Clara de Mowbray may be capital companions as individuals in the abstract: but as "Cook's Tourists" they become an aggregate of terror.'

It did not apparently cross Russell's mind that he, the intrepid foreign correspondent of the Crimea War, was no more or less than a tourist himself. In the early months of 1869 he had accompanied the Prince of Wales to Egypt to observe the breaching of the dam which permitted the waters of the Mediterranean to flow into the Bitter Lakes. From there the entourage had moved on down the Nile to Luxor to stick their heads into malodorous mummy-pits, to gaze in wonder at the Temple at Karnak lit by magnesium flares, to unpack their picnic hampers in the Valley of the Kings, Russell reflecting that to judge from the wall-paintings 'the Pharaoh of 3,000 years ago was not indifferent to creature comforts, though soda-water and ice-making machines were not known to him.'

All in all Russell found Egypt 'most agreeable' and an excellent 'sanitary resort', and gently reproves the policy-makers for letting Egypt go by the run, as he nautically put it. He has nothing but praise for Ismail for his lavish hospitality and merciful rule. The next ten years were to put a new complexion on both of these supposed virtues: in pursuit of lavishness Ismail first mortgaged his country to the European money-lenders, then bankrupted it, so that 'mercy' was transmuted into whip-handed tax-collectors standing over the *fellahin* until they pawned their last trinkets. By the time Ismail the Magnificent was forcibly removed in 1879 Britain had a proprietary interest in the welfare of Egypt (having acquired shares in the Canal, which Ismail sold on the cheap in 1875 to keep abreast of the interest on his debts) which led irresistably in the 1880s to an imperial concern for North and Central Africa. However, in the early 1870s there were plenty of responsible men prepared, like Russell, to take the Khedive at face value.

One of these was Sir Samuel Baker, a brave and compulsive wanderer of the kind Victorian Britain specialized in. He had been in Ceylon, India, the Balkans, and in 1865 had earned his knighthood by battling his way up the Nile as far as Lake Albert. He too had been in the Prince of Wales' party, as interpreter, and during that visit had been invited by the Khedive to lead a military expedition to annex the Upper Nile and suppress the slave trade. 'The Khedive', writes Baker[4], 'was determined to attack that moral cancer [of slavery] by actual cautery at the very root of the evil.'

Cleopatra's Needle (an ancient inscribed monolith) at Alexandria in 1877, awaiting shipment to England in its strange, torpedo-like container. Only after a perilous voyage being towed behind a steamship – and almost foundering in the Bay of Biscay – was the monument finally erected on London's embankment.

That, in retrospect, we have to doubt, for the Khedive could hardly have been unaware that the slave-trade was to a large extent organized by his own officials on a very lucrative basis. However, the appearance of liberalism was important to his European credit, and he was using Baker – as he later used Gordon – to give the veneer of Western respectability to his regime. At all events by the beginning of 1870 Baker (and Lady Baker, who stoically endured the miseries, the malarial swamps, the ambushes of the journey to the bitter end) was ready in Khartoum with three steamboats, two regiments, artillery, sawmills and all the other accoutrements without which a nineteenth-century exploration would have felt naked.

Villages along the Nile were deserted, whole communities consigned to slavery. Arab traders, who clearly had failed to note the day forty years ago when the British government had outlawed slavery, 'rented' thousands of square miles each to pursue their beastly calling, igniting traditional tribal hostilities in order to enslave the losers before turning on the victors. The final disillusion for Baker comes when he discovers his old friend, the governor of Fashoda, is taking a percentage on every slave passing down river on the traders' boats. When finally he comes face to face with one of the most dangerous slave-traffickers of all, Abou Saood, he is stunned by the brazen effrontery of the man. 'He now came to me daily at Fatiko, and swore, by the eyes of the Prophet, eternal fidelity.

British tourists at Luxor. Cook's had begun running conducted tours to Egypt in the late 1860s: the Egyptians responded by illuminating their ruins with magnesium flares for the benefit of sightseers.

He wished to kiss my hand, and to assure me how little his real character had been understood, and that he felt sure I had been influenced against him by others, but that in reality I had no servant so devoted as himself.'

All this while, as Baker well knew, there were upwards of a thousand slaves in the vicinity of Fatiko alone, herded into pens and roped together by the neck. As merchandise their value would increase when they got to Zanzibar (if they survived the hideous journey), but here they were just so much cattle. Less in fact, for it required ten cows for a distraught father to ransom his child, and in the market place a healthy young girl fetched a single elephant's tusk of the first class – or, oddly enough, thirteen English needles.

These were the miserable downcast creatures Baker had come so far to save, and indeed he did succeed in freeing many hundreds of them with his own hand (though it perplexed him when some elected to stay with the traders). When he claimed at the end of his expedition that 'The White Nile, for a distance of 1,600 miles from Khartoum to Central Africa, was cleansed from the abomination of a traffic which had hitherto sullied its waters', he was telling the truth of a sort. The river trade *was* curtailed, yet away from its banks the abomination continued undiminished. Baker's dilemma was that this humanitarian aspect of his expedition was sadly at odds with his second injunction from the Khedive: to bring these unruly tribes under the aegis of Egypt and annex their lands. This paradox clearly did not weigh on Sir Samuel's mind, for he equated the Khedive's protection with salvation from slavery. The tribal chiefs he encountered – when in March 1871 he emerged from the Sudd and pressed on southwards – did not share this view.

To all of them Baker at first made friendly overtures, lavishing on them the currency of the white man's friendship – mirrors, tin whistles, spinning tops – and entertaining them with sherbert and tobacco and, his most successful gambit, his magnetic battery. If things were going well, out would come this monstrous apparatus and the guests would in turn be invited to grasp the two live cylinders in their hands. The sight of so many brave headmen writhing in contortions on the ground was the source of unending merriment, and admiration. At such times Baker made sure his surroundings were as impressive as conditions allowed. In Unyoro he constructed a 'Residence' some twenty-four feet long, hung with blankets and mats and decorated with sporting prints and a life-size picture of the Princess of Wales.

These scenarios did impress the local chieftains, even the headman of Unyoro, Kabba Rega. This powerful leader, whom Baker sadly underestimated as a 'gauche, awkward, undignified lout of twenty years of age' who had beautifully manicured fingernails and tried to walk like a giraffe, came and watched and went away with

his suspicions confirmed. And he was right, of course, for in a very few days Baker (as was his wont) had paraded his men, struck up the band, fired a salute and hoisted the Ottoman flag over all Unyoro territories.

It was an empty gesture: soon the station was besieged by whooping warriors and Baker's little contingent was fighting for its life. Only four men were lost in this battle of Masindi, but the subsequent retreat through the tall grasses back to the Nile was a nightmare, with ambushes every mile – yet Lady Baker acquitted herself nobly with a Colt revolver stuck in her belt and spare ammunition stuffed down her cleavage. The last few months, before the Bakers returned to Cairo in August 1873 to receive the Imperial Order of the Osmanie, 2nd Class, and a fee of £40,000 from the Khedive, were more successful. A permanent station was founded at Fatiko, more slaves rescued, Abou Saood at last arrested, and peace of a sort reigned along the river. It was only after Baker had returned to England that he learned, to his stupefaction, that the Khedive had released Abou Saood and awarded him a lucrative government post.

Granted it was but a freelance enterprise under dubious auspices, Baker's adventure could be interpreted – as indeed it was by some – as a form of proto-colonialism. And the more the continent became 'opened up' in this fashion throughout the 1870s and that hiatus on the African map where the statutory elephant took the place of rivers and mountains was filled, the nearer came that day when the concert of Europe would amicably carve out its various portions. But at the beginning of the decade governments would go to almost any lengths *not* to become embroiled inside Africa. No better example of this could be found than in Britain's slightly weird expedition to Abyssinia in 1868.

This 'minor' intervention, which ultimately involved more than 60,000 men and cost more than £8½ million, was launched with the sole objective of rescuing two British consuls and a collection of fifty-eight other European civilians from the clutches of the demented Emperor Theodore III. It was to some extent the fault of the Foreign Office that they had been incarcerated (for four years) in the mountain fortress of Magdala, for somewhere in the warrens of Whitehall a letter from Theodore to Queen Victoria, dated 1862, had been lost or diplomatically overlooked. The absence of any reply, as months turned into years, threw the Emperor into periodic fits of fury one of which culminated in his chaining up almost every white man, woman and child he could find.

From then on no amount of diplomatic pressure could induce him to free his captives, but the tide of British indignation was rising and the Government was carried reluctantly on its crest. The punitive force under Sir Robert Napier which disgorged itself on to the beach

A daunting but compulsive part of the itinerary: clambering up the pyramids.

201

The Abyssinian war, a 'minor intervention', ultimately confronted the mad Emperor Theodore with the full majesty of the British army, here encamped at Zula. Theodore himself committed suicide just before his mountain fastness at Magdala was overrun.

at Zula in December 1867 included 8,000 camels, 44 elephants, an entire railway system, an electric telegraph unit, nine official photographers, a zoologist, an archaeologist and a bevy of newspaper correspondents. One of these was G. A. Henty, later to become famous for his adventure stories, though he could scarcely have devised a yarn more ripping than the one in which he was now participating[17].

For Henty it began at the beachhead at Zula as all civilized expeditions should start, with champagne and roast beef on Christmas Day. But then as the 400-mile advance got under way in earnest he learnt that all native servants were to be dismissed: 'Their soups are excellent,' he moaned. 'Their cutlets the best I ever tasted, their preserved potatoes baked in cakes delicious. They sent up birds in as good a style as I can get them in a London club. Their pumpkin pie was the talk of the camp; the fame of their baked sheep's head, with brain cutlets, came to the ears of Sir Robert Napier himself.' From then on it was bare rations, the local tedge which tasted like mouldy lemons, honey black with ants, and rum 'in which several cockroaches had committed suicide.'

As Napier's juggernaut moved ponderously towards Magdala Henty recounts in detail the immense difficulties of the march: hoisting cannon up and down 3,000-foot ravines, the decimation of the pack animals through a mysterious high-altitude affliction, the searing thirst, even the baboons who insisted on using the telegraph wire as a trapeze and bringing the whole lot down. He even has time to visit the strange Abyssinian hill-churches en route, and discourse on the extreme moral laxity of the women: 'A virtuous woman is a crown to her husband. I fear there are very few crowned heads in Abyssinia.' Then on Good Friday, 1868 the daunting shape of Magdala is in sight, 'like a three-topped mountain with almost perpendicular sides'.

Hardly have the first baggage-trains come into view than part of Theodore's horde is seen scuttling down the mountainside to attack, thousands of them in scarlet and silk. But it is a terrible error – the mule-trains are not unprotected, as they thought; the Punjabi Pioneers are there, and soon the Naval Brigade, the Madras Sappers and Bombay cavalry – above all the 4th King's Own with their devastating Snider rifles. The unequal battle of Arogee lasted only an hour and a half: Hale's new rockets, together with the withering infantry salvoes and Indian bayonet charges were irresistable. Nearly 2,000 Abyssinian casualties to a mere handful of British. 'The natives', wrote Henty, 'behaved really very gallantly. Not a single shield, gun or spear has been picked up except by the side of the dead. The living, even the wounded, retreated; they did not fly.'

Up in his mountain fastness the mad Emperor was blowing hot and cold, and the fate of his prisoners hung precariously in the balance. At one moment he was falling on his defenceless Abyssinian captives, butchering them right and left with his sword, then hurling them in their thousands down the precipice; the next moment he was praying for forgiveness and attempting (unsuccessfully) to blow his brains in. After the fiasco at Arogee he thought to appease Napier by releasing the Europeans and – miraculously – they were seen trudging out of the fortress, soon to be followed by a mass of deserting warriors, their families and their cows.

But Napier was not to be appeased, and Theodore was obliged to sell his life dear with just a few hundred loyal followers. The final assault was no formality, and the fact that the engineers who had headed the storming party to blow the gate in forgot to take any powder with them did not materially assist matters. But all resistance crumbled away when it was learned that Theodore had finally succeeded in directing a bullet into his own head, and by the evening of Easter Monday the colours of the 33rd had been raised on the mountaintop.

Every aim had now been achieved, at almost no loss of life. A vast kingdom lay at Napier's feet. Yet within two months from the day Magdala fell, there was not so much as a trace of this huge expedition left on Abyssinian soil. No one even hinted that the army should stay there, indeed the whole episode had simply gone to prove, as the *Illustrated London News* put it, 'how necessary it is to keep ourselves clear from political contact with nations that are not yet sufficiently advanced in civilization to conform to the canons of international good faith and decorous demeanour. Government will, we trust . . . firmly resist being dragged into political relations with barbarous chieftains.'

Henry Morton Stanley (centre) photographed at Zanzibar in the mid-1880s.

One of those foreign correspondents who had witnessed the storming of Magdala, and indeed had inspected the mortal remains of Theodore after its fall, was Henry Morton Stanley, the representative of the

New York Herald. His name was not then a by-word in the homes of Britain and America, for three years were to pass before he was to march into Ujiji and 'discover' Livingstone 'a mere ruckle of bones'. But he had at last set foot on the continent which was to claim him body and soul for the next twenty years. More than any others, perhaps, it was his accounts of Central Africa that were to ignite men's imagination about this darkest of continents.

This Welsh orphan, who had run away to America as a lad and been adopted by an American benefactor, was a born buccaneer. He had fought (on both sides) in the American Civil War, and had since roamed the world from Colorado to Constantinople in search of a story. In 1874 he persuaded the *Daily Telegraph* and *New York Herald* to sponsor an attempt to circumnavigate the great Central Lakes and to continue the work of Livingstone (whose death had just been reported) on the Lualaba river. When news of his expedition became public, he says in his book[27], he was inundated with offers of assistance from all over Europe many of which (ironically for a race which professed a higher civilization than the savages of the interior) put at his disposal powers that guaranteed the success of the venture: one promised to put all inimicable tribes to sleep, another to give the expedition wings, yet another to make it invisible!

But Stanley had no need of these magic arts. His tactics were more straightforward: fight your way out of trouble. On his two-and-a-half-year journey he fought no less than thirty-two pitched battles, lost every white man who accompanied him, and arrived at the mouth of the Congo in 1877 with less than a third of his expedition intact. Time and again he confides to his diary his despair at the constant slaughter: 'It is a murderous world, and we feel for the first time that we hate the filthy, vulturous ghouls who inhabit it.' And a little later: 'At every curve of this fearful river the yells of the savages broke loud on our ears . . . there were not thirty in the entire expedition that had not received a wound. To continue this fearful life was not possible. Some day we should lie down and offer our throats like lambs to the cannibal butchers.' Each time the meat escaped the butchers, but then there was some fearful cataract to contend with, or hideous tropical ulcers that could gnaw a man's foot to the bone. In hostile country Stanley had no time, and less inclination, to inspect the tribes around him; but where the natives came in friendship to him, he responded with typical Victorian magnanimity.

One amenable monarch proved to be Chumbiri, ruler of Uyanzi, whose wives caught Stanley's fancy for the huge collars of brass, some 30lb each, soldered round their necks as a token of their husband's status. He estimated Chumbiri thus possessed a portable store of 1,400lb of brass, though was less than amused when the king demonstrated how he rescued his hoard from the neck of a dead wife, by leeringly drawing his finger across his throat. Equally friendly

were the Babwende, amongst whom he was astonished to find examples of Delft ware and Birmingham cutlery. By enquiry he was able to unravel some of the complexities of the internal trading system along the Congo, coming to the conclusion that one ancient Portuguese musket (presumably traded by the earliest European settlers on the coast) had taken 390 years to be bartered as far as this tribe.

Mtesa, the potent king of Uganda (whom Speke had known for a vicious rogue who made sport of murdering his wives), in particular became a devoted ally. Stanley found him much mellowed and 'interested in the discussion of the manners and customs of European courts, and to be enamoured of hearing the wonders of civilization. He is ambitious to imitate as much as lies in his power the ways of the white man.' The explorer was much disturbed to learn that the king had (through the influence of Arab slave-traders) embraced Mohammet, and dedicated several weeks to weaning him to Christianity by translating large chunks of the scriptures into Swahili.

Sadly for Stanley's good works, by 1883, when the young Scottish explorer Joseph Thomson approached Mtesa's kingdom from the south-east through Kenya, the novelty of Christianity had worn thin and the blood-lust of Mtesa's youth had reasserted itself in grisly fashion. Thomson himself, deputed to lead a Royal Geographical Society expedition through the territories of the dreaded Masais at the tender age of 26, wisely refrained from proselytizing amongst the tribes he encountered. Indeed he confined himself to dispensing charms and magic potions – the most efficacious of which he found to be Eno's Fruit Salts, which bubbled up the noses of delighted chieftains who then retired convinced of their invulnerability against the spears of their enemies.

Thomson's cautious approaches, so unlike Stanley's blockbusting, enabled him to return with fascinating, first-hand descriptions of tribal customs[31]: the toilet of a Mteita damsel, 'a coating of lamp black and castor-oil, which emits an aroma that gallantry compels me to call pleasing, but which as an aside to the reader, I confess to be simply awful'; the ear-stretching and female circumcision of the Masai (a barbarous practice which Thomson felt obliged, for the sensibilities of his readers, to describe in Latin). He was also an enthusiastic photographer, and returned with some valuable material – though sometimes even his undoubted charms failed to allay the superstitions. 'In vain did I appeal to their love of gaudy ornaments... the moment the attempt to focus them took place they would fly in terror to the shelter of the woods. They imagined I was a magician trying to take possession of their souls, which once accomplished they would be entirely at my mercy.'

Reports from deepest Africa like Stanley's served to strengthen, if anything, Britain's resolve not to shoulder the burden of any more uncharted and primitive expanses of the world's surface. Already the Empire struck many intelligent imperialists as unwieldy, expensive and vulnerable. In 1873, even before Stanley set off, an episode on the Gold Coast (present-day Ghana) had demonstrated just how expensive and vulnerable it could be in the most unlikely areas. Now that the slave-markets on the west coast of Africa had all but died out, British presence on the feverish Gold Coast had little, beyond a trickle of trade, to commend it. To the Ashanti, the pre-eminent African imperialists of the interior, there was even less to commend it, for the obstinate foreigner continued to deny them access to the sea. In 1872 their Asantahene, King Kofi (more ribaldly known as King Coffee) had the impertinence to put the issue to the test by attacking two white outposts at Elmina and Cape Coast. British revenge the following year was swift and terrible – a textbook example, by the up-and-coming Sir Garnet Wolseley, of how to conduct a minor colonial war. It had ended predictably with the utter destruction of Kofi's sacred capital at Kumasi, but not before an indelible and appalling impression had been stamped on the memories of those who penetrated it: the stench, bones and blood of human sacrifice had assailed them on all sides – reinforcing the conviction that wherever Britain's mission lay, it was not in Africa's squalid hinterland.

The opencast diamond mine workings at Kimberley, 1871. Each small rectangular plot represents a claim of an individual prospector or company.

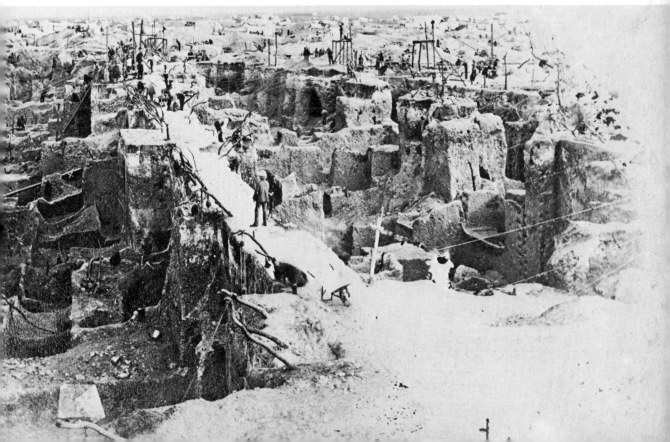

But events in Africa followed their own logic. As in Abyssinia in
1868, as in Ashantiland in 1873, the British in South Africa had no
enthusiasm for imposing themselves on what the Government agent
in Basutoland called 'the most God-lost looking ruffians that I ever
beheld in my life.' (One cannibal he was introduced to claimed to
have 'captured during one of his hunting expeditions three young
women. From these he selected the best-looking as his partner for
life. The other two went to stock his larder.') That was in 1868 when
two colonies, Natal and Cape Colony, were considered sufficient for
the purpose of exercising a mandate over the important sea route
round the Cape – however unprepossessing they might have been.
The Revd Milner, accompanying the Duke of Edinburgh to Cape
Town on an official tour in 1867[21], found the colony 'in indifferent
circumstances; a cattle plague, a disease amongst the sheep, the grape
disease and overspeculation among the mercantile community had
more or less involved all classes in distress, in many cases to the verge
of ruin.'

The other two provinces of South Africa further inland were Boer
republics, the Orange Free State and the Transvaal, whither the
stern, bible-packing Dutchmen had trekked in earlier years to escape
the influence of British colonialism. They were no better off than
their English neighbours – indeed the Transvaal was popularly
believed to be a disaster-area. Anthony Trollope, reporting on a
private inspection in 1878[37], was only echoing the feelings of Whitehall

succintly, if a shade too bluntly when he commented: '. . . slavery was rampant. The natives were being encouraged to rebellion. The president was impotent. The Volksraad was stiff-necked and ignorant. There was no revenue, no order, no obediance. The Dutch seemed to have forgotten even the way to fight.'

Trollope, one need hardly add, had little regard for Boers. 'The Boers are at present much abused for cowardice. . . I fear that of late there has been truth in these stories and that the pluck shewn by them when they made good their hold upon the country has been greatly dimmed by the quiet uneventful tenor of their present lives.' This attitude was one which permeated the entire British consciousness. 'Let an Englishman be where he may about the surface of the globe, he always thinks himself superior to other men around him. He eats more, drinks more, wears more clothes and both earns and spends more money. He – and the American who in this respect is the same as an Englishman – always consumes the wheat while others put up with the rye.' So observed Trollope, and went on to reflect that this attitude in South Africa particularly 'produces something akin to contempt. There is no English farmer in South Africa who would not feel himself vilified by being put on a par with a Dutch farmer.' And, in due course, it was in this frame of mind that Britain lurched into its most humiliating war of the era.

The overture came in 1877, when the Government found it had actually annexed the Transvaal, without explicit orders to Sir Theophilus Shepstone, its special commissioner, to do so (or not to do so, for that matter, so hedged about with qualifications was his brief). The fact was that in the early seventies the great interior had begun to assume an unforeseen importance, as reports from Kimberley, Namaqualand, from beyond the Vaal filtered back to the coast of an eldorado of diamonds, gold and copper waiting to be plundered. And with each mule train that arrived with fresh communiqués, new waves of prospectors hurled themselves upon the veldt, oblivious to the encircling menace of the volatile Tembu, Zulu, Basutos and Griquas. Already the fragile edifice of the Transvaal republic was being assaulted by the native chief Secocoeni, and defeat could easily open up the floodgates to a black inundation that could wash every white settler into the sea. The refusal in 1879 of the Zulu king, Cetewayo, to disband his armies according to Britain's instructions seemed to be yet one more justification for the annexation and for a strong, united white South Africa under Queen Victoria.

Cetewayo's flying squadrons, with their assegais and spine-chilling war chants, were most undesirable neighbours to live with, and when their blood was up they had scant respect for breech-loading rifles or bayonets. One British force under Lord Chelmsford, sent to enforce the disarmament ultimatum, was utterly annihilated at Isandhlwana, and national pride restored only by the heroic defence

Overleaf: Zulu maidens in seductive pose, 1870s.

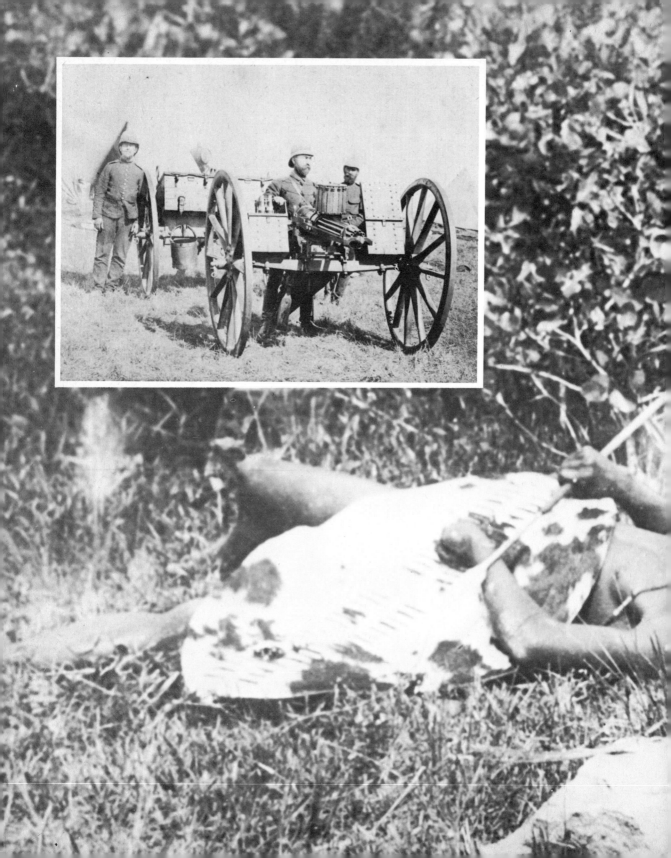

A fallen Zulu warrior, 1879. Zulus, with their flying columns and chilling war-cries, proved formidable opponents – if no match, in the final analysis, for the Gatling gun batteries (inset) of the British army.

of Rorke's Drift (just a field hospital and a few huts) by literally a handful of Welshmen against 4,000 suicidal Zulus. Eleven Victoria Crosses were won that day (22 January 1879) which, with every justification, entered the military mythology of the thin red line to be glorified in odes and oilpaint. From that point on the Zulu star had set, for the full regimental majesty of the British army now arrayed itself against the savage and methodically destroyed him. (Defeated, Cetewayo ceased to be a savage and assumed the status of sporting opponent, to be magnanimously welcomed in London three years later).

Such a campaign, of course, would have been far beyond the re-sources of the Boers. Shepstone, when he'd read out his proclamation of annexation in the main square of Pretoria, had been correct in assessing the republic as bankrupt and ill-managed, but he'd been wrong in one important particular: that it followed therefore that the Boers wished to fly to the bosom of Britannia and accept her embrace. Shepstone produced trumped-up 'petitions' to indicate that they did, but even Trollope was unconvinced by them: 'They show the energy of the instigators of the petition and not of the petitioners. . . It is as though a strong boy should say to a weak one "It is better that I should have your cricket bat than you" and should therefore take it.' Plenty of others at home thought it wasn't cricket either at the time, notably Mr Gladstone who expressed himself so forcibly against this kind of gunboat imperialism, during his famous whistle-stop election campaign in Midlothian (1879), that he was plunged into office almost in a trough of national guilt.

But it was not as convenient, to Gladstone in office, to offer the Boers back their independence as swiftly as he had hinted at in opposition. By the autumn of 1880 they were still waiting, and exceedingly impatient. Came December and a frontiersman by the name of Paul Kruger, a diehard fundamentalist of the most intractible kind, resolved to take Deuteronomy literally when it enjoined 'when thou comest nigh unto a city fight against it'. On 30 December the Transvaal Boers unilaterally declared themselves a republic under Kruger, and prepared to defend their right to do so. It so happened

Farmers turned guerillas:
Transvaal Boers in 1881.

that the occupying forces in Transvaal had been run down to the
barest minimum – but this did not bother the new High Commissioner of South Africa, Sir George Colley, overmuch since he
subscribed even more tenaciously than Trollope to the dictum that
the Boers were mortal cowards. He continued to hold to it when at
Bronkhurst Spruit the Boers, using unorthodox (not to say ungentle-
manly) guerrilla tactics, decimated a British column. Nor would he
relinquish it when the farmers made a mockery of his invading army
at Laing's Nek at the end of January. And doubtless he still clung to
it as he was shot down on top of Majuba Hill the next month, defending a useless outcrop of rock against their deadly and demoralizing
rifle fire. By April the Boers had officially shaken off their irksome
colonial yoke but, strangely, they found it a great deal harder to
shake Britain's low opinion of their fighting qualities. In 1899, as
on this occasion, the army stumbled into a 'tea-time' war with them
in the same misguided belief that it would be all over by supper.

The Travellers and their Books

The numbers beside each entry correspond with the numbered references throughout the text.

Avonmore, Viscountess: *Theresina in America* (1875) 1

Baden Powell, George: *New Homes for the Old Country* (1872) 2

Baker, James: *Turkey in Europe* (1877) 3

Baker, Sir Samuel: *Expedition to Central Africa to Suppress the Slave Trade* (1874) 4

Carnegie, Andrew: *American Four-in-hand* (1881) 6

Daily News: *Correspondence of War* (1871) 7

Doré, Gustave (and Blanchard Jerrold): *London – A Pilgrimage* (1872) 8

Dresser, Dr Christopher: *Art and Art-manufactures of Japan* (1878) 9

Dufferin and Ava, Marchioness of: *Canadian Journal 1872–78* 10

Evans, Arthur: *Through Bosnia and Herzegovina on Foot* (1876) 11

FitzGibbon, Mary: *A Trip to Manitoba* (1880) 12

Forbes, Archibald: *Adventures of a British Lad in the Russo-Turkish War of 1877–78* 13

Forrest, John: *Explorations in Australia* (1875) 14

Fraser, Mrs Hugh: *A Diplomatist's Wife in Many Lands 1868–81* 15

Gay, Drew: *From Pall Mall to the Punjab* (1876) 16

Henty, G. A.: *The March to Magdala* (1868) 17

James, Henry: *English Hours 1877–81* 18, *Parisian Sketches 1875–76* 19

La Meslée, Edmond Marin: *The New Australia* (1833) 20

Milner, Revd John (and Oswald Brierly): *The Cruise of HMS* Galatea (1869) 21

Nightingale, Florence: *The People of India* (1877) 22

Orr, Mrs Sutherland: *The Future of Englishwomen* (1877) 23

Russell, William Howard: *Diary in the East* (1869) 24

Sala, George Augustus: *Journey Due South* (1881) 25, *America Re-visited* (1882) 26

Stanley, Henry Morton: *Through the Dark Continent* (1878) 27

Stevenson, Robert Louis: *Travels with a Donkey* (1879) 28

Seward, William Henry: *Travels around the World* (1873) 29

Thomson, John: *The Straits of Mallacca, Cochin-China and China* (1874) 30

Thomson, Joseph: *Through Masai Land* (1885) 31

Troubridge, Laura: *Journals of a Young Victorian 1873–84* 32

Twain, Mark: *Innocents Abroad* (1875), 34 *A Tramp Abroad* (1880) 36

Trollope, Anthony: *South Africa* (1878) 37

Vincent, Mrs Howard: *Forty Thousand Miles over Land and Water* (1886) 38

Williamson, Revd Alexander: *Journeys in Northern China* (1870) 39

Wellesley, Col. F. A.: *With the Russians in Peace and War* (1871–78) 40

Williams, Prof. Monier: *Modern India* (1878) 41

Anon: *London, Wonderful London* (1878) 43

Journals

The Times, Illustrated London News, Punch, Pall Mall Gazette, Fortnightly Review, Nineteenth Century, The New York Times, The Californian

The Photographers

Index

*Page references in italics
refer to captions to illustrations.*

Acknowledgements

The publishers are grateful to the following for supplying illustrations:

Archiv für Kunst und Geschichte: 57, 99; Australian Information Service: 128, 137, 138–9; The Bancroft Library, Univ. of California: 118; The Bettman Archive: 93; California Historical Society: 114t; Coffrin's Old West Gallery: 109; Culver Pictures Inc: 96b; Dr Barnardo's: 14; Eastman Photographic Collection: 107, 114–15; Frank Meadow Sutcliffe: 36–7, 39t, 39b, 40; George Sirot: 53; Gernsheim Collection: 24, 26, 27, 32, 32 inset, 45, 47, 59, 63, 67, 68, 75, 89, 90–91, 94, 110 inset, 186–7; Greater London Council: 15, 17, 28t, 28b, 29, 197; Guildhall Library: 11; India Office: 176, 178, 181, 184–5, 185, 187, 190–91; Kingston-upon-Thames Corporation: 33t; Kodak Museum: 56, 133b; Library of Congress: 102, 103, 110–11; Mansell Collection: 13, 18, 19, 37, 49, 193; Minnesota Historical Society: 108t; The Mitchell Library: 131, 132–3, 134t, 134b, 142, 143; Montana Historical Society: 106; Museum of the City of New York: 96t, 98; National Army Museum: 216, 216 inset, 218; Notman Collection: 121, 122–3, 125t; Österreichische Nationalbibliothek: 65; Staatsbibliothek Preussischer Kulturbesitz: 51; Post Office: 35t; Public Archives Canada: 126t; Radio Times Hulton Picture Library: 2–3, 21, 31, 44, 48, 50–51, 73, 84–5, 85 inset, 87b, 104, 126b, 161, 167, 186, 194, 198, 200, 205; Robert Sheridan: 83; Roger-Viollet: 42, 60–61, 66; Royal Geographical Society: 77, 80, 81, 116t, 125, 144, 146, 147, 148, 149, 150t, 150b, 151, 153, 154, 155, 156–7, 158–9, 180, 188, 202–3, 206, 208–9; The Royal Library: 189, 212; Royal Photographic Society: 9, 16, 22; Science Museum: 120; Solomon D. Butcher: 108b, 114b; State Library of South Australia: 140–41; US Department of the Interior: 101; Victoria & Albert Museum: 70–71, 163, 165, 168–9, 170–71, 172–3, 176, 182–3, 211, 214–15.

The photographs on pages 189 and 212 are reproduced by gracious permission of Her Majesty the Queen.